C000058360

Tales from the Big House:
Temple Newsam

For Linda

Tales from the
Big House:
Temple Newsam

The Hampton Court of the North, 1,000 years of its History and People

Steve Ward

PEN & SWORD
HISTORY

First published in Great Britain in 2017 by
Pen & Sword History
an imprint of
Pen & Sword Books Ltd
47 Church Street
Barnsley
South Yorkshire
S70 2AS

Copyright © Steve Ward 2017

ISBN 978 1 47389 335 1

The right of Steve Ward to be identified as the Author of this Work has
been asserted by him in accordance with the Copyright, Designs and
Patents Act 1988.

A CIP catalogue record for this book is available from the
British Library

All rights reserved. No part of this book may be reproduced or
transmitted in any form or by any means, electronic or mechanical
including photocopying, recording or by any information storage and
retrieval system, without permission from the Publisher in writing.

Typeset in Ehrhardt by
Mac Style Ltd, Bridlington, East Yorkshire
Printed and bound in the UK by CPI Group (UK) Ltd,
Croydon, CR0 4YY

Pen & Sword Books Limited incorporates the imprints of Atlas,
Archaeology, Aviation, Discovery, Family History, Fiction, History,
Maritime, Military, Military Classics, Politics, Select, Transport,
True Crime, Air World, Frontline Publishing, Leo Cooper,
Remember When, Seaforth Publishing, The Praetorian Press,
Wharncliffe Local History, Wharncliffe Transport,
Wharncliffe True Crime and White Owl

For a complete list of Pen & Sword titles please contact
PEN & SWORD BOOKS LIMITED
47 Church Street, Barnsley, South Yorkshire, S70 2AS, England
E-mail: enquiries@pen-and-sword.co.uk
Website: www.pen-and-sword.co.uk

Contents

Acknowledgements

I n compiling this book I have received help and support from many people. Although they are far too numerous to mention in full, I would specifically like to thank the following:

Rachel Conroy, Curator of Temple Newsam House; Kitty Ross, Curator of the Abbey House Museum; Lucy Moore, Projects Curator for Leeds Museums; Lord Halifax; Julie Holroyd and Adrian Thompson, Visitor Assistants at Temple Newsam House; Derek Voller; Lis Burke; Neil Clifton; Richard Thomson; David Pacey; The West Yorkshire Archive Service; The Borthwick Institute; The Thoresby Society; Imperial War Museums, London; The British Red Cross Archives; The Shakespeare Birthplace Trust Archives; The Leeds Library; The Royal Archives; Heritage Technology Ltd; members of the general public and, of course, my wife Linda – for her endless patience.

Foreword

A student of mine once said to me that history is boring and what is the need to study it? It is only about dead people and the past; we should be looking to the future. Well, I would argue differently. History is all around us and we cannot escape from it. What we do today is history in the making; the future is history that has not yet happened. We are all part of history; it is that giant tapestry upon which we weave our own individual stories. History is not dead; it is very much still alive. Einstein once said that the concept of the past, present and future is only an illusion – however persistent. If we follow his theories, however complex they may seem, we can understand that, on the space-time continuum, the past has not gone and neither is the future non-existent. The past, present and future can all exist in the same way.

This is all very well for scientists but most people live their lives in the now and consider the past to be gone and no longer existent. But let me try to give an example: you visit a friend one evening and then you say goodbye and leave. That goodbye still exists as a moment in time even though physically you may have moved on in time and space. You can still revisit that moment in your memory or, if that moment was photographed or filmed, via that medium also; the moment still exists for you and that 'historical' moment (for it *has* happened) is still alive. This works of course if an event happens within your living memory or within a period subsequent to the invention of a recording medium. But there are other tangible ways in which history can still be alive – through artefacts and buildings.

The other day I spent time in an archive handling and reading letters from the seventeenth century. Someone all those years ago had taken up their pen, dipped it into ink and written those words on that paper. As I read them I shared the moment of 'nowness' with the writers; their 'now' and my 'now' had coincided at that point. It is the same principle with buildings and other structures. If you visit Temple Newsam, and I sincerely hope that you will, place your hand on a brick in an outer wall. Consider that brick was made by someone, loaded and carried to Temple Newsam by another and then laid by yet another person. As you touch that brick, you momentarily share a common 'nowness' with all those people who may have handled that brick in one way or another. Similarly when inside the house, pause for a moment and consider who has walked that piece of floor before you, and who has stood in that room you are standing in. As you walk through the house think of the people who may have lived or worked there; people who laughed and cried, argued and made love, and children who ran about. Listen to the house and get a feeling of that. If you allow your now and their now to meet, however briefly, then you will experience the livingness of history.

We are blessed in Britain in that we have so many organisations dedicated to preserving our heritage. Some are very well known, such as Historic England, English Heritage and the National Trust. Others are perhaps a little less well known but equally important – the Ancient Monument Society and the Gardens Trust, for example. Some are focused on particular periods, such as the Georgian Society and the Victorian Society, and others are dedicated to specific buildings or skills, such as the Theatres Trust or the British Institution of Organ Studies. Across the British Isles we have countless monuments to our past, including castles, monasteries, churches, cathedrals, country houses and stately homes. Some are maintained and preserved by government funding or through charities, and others are still privately owned. For visitors it seems that you need not have travelled but a short distance before you stumble across some ancient edifice erected to the glory of a bygone age. Yet each one has a different story to tell.

This is just the case with Temple Newsam House and Estate. Standing only a few miles from Leeds in West Yorkshire, it is now a quiet haven of tranquillity where many visitors come to picnic or stroll through the extensive grounds and admire the beauty of the house. But I wonder how many actually take the time to stop to think about who has walked the ground before them?

Temple Newsam has a long history, almost one thousand years of it, dating back to before the time of the Norman Conquest and long before the current house was built, or even the name used. Temple Newsam House celebrates its 500th anniversary in 2018. Throughout its time it has survived wars, plagues and social upheaval. But a house is just bricks and mortar, and whilst we can learn much from the architecture, the true story of a house lies with the people who lived in it, and Temple Newsam is no different. Many people have lived, worked and died in the house during its existence. Some have been illustrious, some notorious and some as ordinary as you and me. Some of those names we may instantly recognise – Lancelot 'Capability' Brown, Lord Darnley, and Joseph Priestley to name but a few; others have been lost in the mists of time but are, nonetheless, equally fascinating.

This book is not intended as a guide book and neither is it an academic history. It will be, I hope, a good and interesting read; one of those books that you like to 'dip into' to find out more about something or somewhere you thought you already knew about. For those of you who know of and have visited Temple Newsam before, I hope that it will help you find something new. For those who have never visited, I very much hope that this book will whet your appetite and make you want to discover for yourself a jewel in the crown of British country houses.

Steve Ward, 2017

Introduction

I f you drive along the M1 motorway, between junctions 43 and 44, take a glance to the west and you might just catch a fleeting glimpse of a rather grand building nestling among the trees on the skyline. There are no signs for it from the motorway, and in my opinion there should be, for this is Temple Newsam House, one of the most impressive and historically important houses in the north of England.

Situated only about 4 miles south-east of the bustling cosmopolitan city of Leeds, Temple Newsam House is a Tudor-Jacobean jewel set in 1,500 acres (370 hectares) of rolling parkland, woodland, lakes and gardens. Today the estate is open as a public park and you can meander at your leisure through most of it. As you do so you will find that the scenery is constantly changing. To the south of the house are more formal gardens, laid out in geometrical lines, but to the east you can wander the rhododendron-flanked paths of the Pleasure Garden, which opens up onto a vista of the Menagerie Ponds – three lakes located before a dramatic hillside backdrop of woodland. The lower lake is set in parkland, the middle lake is fringed with damp loving perennials including hostas, ligularia and yellow flags, and the top lake is bordered by a variety of bamboos. The woodland behind is the second largest part of the original Forest of Leeds, and there are fifty-five units of existing woodland throughout the metropolitan district. The Forest of Leodis was a fifth-century forested area in the kingdom of Elmet and it is from this that the name Leeds was derived.

If you cross the connected lakes by one of the two bridges you have a choice of direction to take. Bear left and you will discover a flight of steps leading to a walled garden. Created in the eighteenth century, this contains over 800 metres (500 yards) of herbaceous borders. Until 1922, all fruit and vegetables for the estate were grown here. After this time it became the home for a short-lived menagerie but it has subsequently been re-landscaped back to its more original form and is now a pleasant place to sit and relax, with many benches provided for visitors. Running the length of the northern wall of the garden is a hothouse, containing a variety of exotic and temperate plants. The Temple Newsam gardens are many and varied, and the estate holds six national plant collections: Phlox, Delphinium, Chrysanthemum, Aster, Primula and Solenostemon.

If you bear right after crossing the bridge you can take one of the many paths that lead upwards into the woodland. Many are bordered by the now invasive rhododendron, which make a dramatic and colourful display in the height of summer. At the top of the slope you may have taken the path that leads to a small Greek temple, known as the 'Little Temple'. Built as a folly during the eighteenth century landscaping of the grounds, it offers a magnificent view across the lakes towards the house. Although now fenced off due to its poor state of repair, it provides a welcome point to stop to catch your breath after the fairly steep climb from the lakes below and to admire the view. Contrary to what one elderly transatlantic lady visitor was overheard to have said about the Little Temple ('I guess this is the reason they called it Temple Newsam'), the property's name existed long before the eighteenth century. Venture further eastwards and narrow paths will lead you through deciduous woodland carpeted with ferns and other shade loving plants. Although the boundaries are never clear, you can wander through Elm and Oak Wood, Dawson's Wood, Avenue Wood, Hertford Springs, and Laurel Hill Wood – all are part of the estate. Wildlife abounds, although you may not always see it. The woods are home to foxes, badgers, bats, and a large variety of birds, including the majestic red kite; even deer have been seen on the fringes of the woodland.

Bisecting Hertford Springs and Dawson's Wood is a grassed carriage drive known as The Avenue, which leads from the eastern boundary of the estate at Bullerthorpe Lane to Temple Newsam House. It is approximately 1 mile in length. From the entrance gates, where once stood a pair of gatehouses that were demolished in 1946, the house is not immediately seen, as the ground rises ahead, but once this ridge is gained a splendid glimpse of the house is seen in the distance between the trees. The drive drops to cross a stone-built bridge spanning the Avenue Ponds before sweeping right, and then the full impact of the house can be seen; a view designed to impress visitors.

If you follow this drive all the way back to the house you will find, just to the east, a neoclassical stable block. Near this there once stood a riding school, now long since demolished, which is shown in a 1745 painting by James Chapman. The painting can be seen today in Temple Newsam House. Beyond the stable block is Home Farm. There has been a farm here certainly since the seventeenth century, and the great barn dates from 1694. Throughout the centuries, a range of other buildings were added to the farm: the cow byre, the saw mill, the engine shed, and the dovecote, which can house more than 1,000 pairs of breeding birds. Home Farm is still a working farm but now it is one of the largest Rare Breed Centres in Europe. It has a variety of native UK breeds of farm animals that are classed as rare breeds by the Rare Breeds Survival Trust (www.rbst.org.uk), including Gloucestershire Old Spot pigs, Norfolk Horn sheep, Bagot goats and Saddleback pigs. Most of these are on display to the public and it is a popular place to visit, for young and old alike.

Temple Newsam is an estate for all seasons. No matter what time of year you visit, you will find something different to look at. Many visitors are not aware of the full story of the place. The house has witnessed much during the last 500 years of the estate's life, but this was not the beginning of Temple Newsam. In fact, the history of the land can be traced back to the times before the Norman invasion, almost 1,000 years ago.

Chapter 1

A Monastic House

How Newsam achieved the title of 'Temple'

Until William the Conqueror invaded Britain in 1066, the land that now comprises the Temple Newsam estate was known to have been controlled by Gluniar and Dunstan, Anglo-Saxon thanes. Before the time of the conquest, Dunstan's name is associated with nine settlements in the current West Yorkshire, and Gluniar's name with seventeen settlements in both the West and North Yorkshire areas; clearly they were important men. In 1085, William ordered a survey of England to be carried out. We know the results of this today as the Domesday Book. In a desire to know as much as he could about the land he had conquered, the Domesday Book was a complete inventory of Britain up to the river Tyne, and gave William power through knowledge. With all this documentation he was, as Simon Schama calls him, 'the first database king' (2000). The book was produced the following year, in 1086, and (Temple) Newsam makes it appearance as 'Neuhusū'. The Tenant in Chief of that settlement was Ilbert de Lacy. The two brothers Walter and Ilbert de Lacy had travelled to England with William and both had subsequently been granted lands for their part in the conquest. Walter had lands in Herefordshire and Shropshire, and Ilbert had lands in Yorkshire and parts of what is now Lancashire.

At the time of the survey, Neuhusū was quite a small place with only ten households – eight villagers and two freemen. The settlement included four ploughlands, enough for three men's plough teams to work on. There were also 3 acres of meadows and half a league of woodland. The tax assessment for Neuhusū was for eight geld units, where a geld was the amount of tax assessed per hide. A hide had been a nominal unit of land measurement equivalent to approximately 120 acres, but the true understanding of the hide unit has been lost in antiquity. Stenton (1971) explains: 'Despite the work of many great scholars, the hide of early English texts remains a term of elusive meaning.'

A hide appears to have been used more as a means of tax assessment rather than as a measurement of land as the nominal figure given was likely to have been different in different locations. With particular reference to the Domesday Book, Dr Sally Harvey, in her 1987 work *Taxation and the Economy*, suggests that a hide of land was worth £1, or land producing £1 worth of income be assessed at one hide. For Neuhusū to have a relatively small population, the tax assessment of eight geld units seems quite high, perhaps suggesting that the productivity of the land was good.

We have to thank the Crusades in the Holy Land for the addition of the word 'Temple' to Newsam. In the aftermath of the first Crusade in 1099, many pilgrims wished to travel to Jerusalem and other holy sites. This was still a dangerous land and many on pilgrimage lost their possessions and their lives at the hands of lawless thieves and murderers. To counter this, in 1119 a French knight, Hugues de Payens, proposed creating a monastic order of knights to protect these pilgrims. This was granted, and the newly formed Poor Fellow Soldiers of Christ and the Temple of Solomon were provided with a base on the site of the captured Al-Aqsa mosque in Jerusalem, believed to have been built on the site of the biblical Temple of Solomon. This small group of knights soon became known as the Order of the Knights Templar and many of us may be familiar with their uniform of a white tabard emblazoned with a red cross.

Feared by many for their ferocity in battle, the Order grew quickly, both in size and wealth. Within a decade of its creation, the Order was the most favoured charity in the Christian world and received many gifts and donations of money, land and business. Members took a vow of poverty and handed over their wealth and possessions to the Order, thereby swelling its coffers. Soon they were able to establish a successful network of commerce, dealing with monarchs, the aristocracy, and the Muslim world. Their fleet of ships in the Mediterranean Sea allowed swift and secure communications between Europe and the Holy Land. The Order strengthened its bases, and in 1139, Pope Innocent II issued a Papal Bull, *Omne Datum Optimum*, exempting the Templars from all local laws and making them answerable only to the Pope himself. This gave members of the Order free rite of passage across all borders and an exemption from paying taxes. The Templars rapidly developed into a very wealthy, powerful and influential body. From their fortified sites in the Holy Land they could provide shelter and safe passage for pilgrims. In addition to this they also acted as early private 'bankers'. Pilgrims could leave their valuables with the Templars, who would issue a receipt in the form of a note of credit, very much like a modern-day money order. This meant that pilgrims were able to travel unencumbered by valuable goods and money. If they did need some of their funds they could present their credit note at the next Templar site. Of course, the Templars took a percentage of a pilgrim's wealth in return for this service, again adding to their growing wealth.

Although particularly strong throughout continental Europe, the Templars gained a foothold in England. At the Order's peak there were thought to be about sixty Templar sites within England, Scotland and Ireland. Each would have been controlled by a preceptor who had responsibility for any knights and brethren within the preceptory. There were in fact very few actual knights in the Order compared to lay brethren. The local preceptories would have been grouped together under a regional priory. According to the *History of the County of York* in the *Victoria County History* series (1974), in about 1155 the land around the area of Neuhusū, including the neighbouring settlements at Colton, Skelton and Whitkirk, was granted to the Knights Templar by William de Villiers and confirmed by the Baron of Pontefract, Henry de Lacy, 'for the salvation of my soul'. Henry was grandson of Ilbert de Lacy, the first Tenant in Chief of Neuhusū. The land then became known as the Preceptory of Temple Newsam and hence the name remains today. Take a look at the index in a Leeds street atlas and you will find ten thoroughfares in the immediate area of Temple Newsam with the name Templar or Temple Newsam and thirty-nine other instances of the use of Temple as a street name.

The Preceptory of Temple Newsam was situated not where the present house stands – that is a much later building – but approximately half a mile to the south, near the river Aire. In 1185, it was listed as having sixteen carucates of land with a value of just under £10. The National Archives gives this an equivalent value of just under £5,500. A carucate of land was estimated as the area that a plough team of eight oxen could plough in a season and is often referred to as a ploughland in the Domesday Book. So we can see that in the hundred years since the Domesday Book was produced, the area of the estate had doubled in size. A 1991 archaeological dig found evidence of a great barn, some 45 metres in length, and other farm buildings to the south of the present house. There were also stone pits that may have been used for tanning hides. Pre-1991 Ordnance Survey maps show this area being partly occupied by Temple Thorpe farm, very near junction 45 of the M1 motorway. Any other archaeological evidence was destroyed in the 1940s by opencast mining and it is thought that the Templar chapel lies under an industrial waste tip to the south. Although there is evidence of the farmstead belonging to the preceptory, the actual whereabouts of the Templar house is not known. One theory offered is that the twelfth-century foundations were incorporated into the building of the north wing of the current house. If this is so then it would mean that the original Templar house occupied the same imposing position that the current one does. There is some logic to this as the Templars maintained the church at Whitkirk, a short distance to the north, and a house situated between the farmstead to the south and the church to the north would have been convenient.

The main occupation of the Order seems to have been sheep farming, although other livestock was also kept. A 1311 survey, taken during the time of the suppression of the Order, showed that the preceptory held the following (P. Robinson, 1926): 44 plough oxen, 14 plough horses, 454 sheep, 335 wethers, and 247 lambs, all to a stock value of £95. In addition to this, the holdings included a chapel, kitchen, dormitories, hall, brewhouse, furnace, dairies and a grange.

With the farmstead being very near the river Aire, it is quite possible that this Templar community exported fleece and wool down the river to the Humber, where Cistercian monks had a community at Hull. They were indeed a wealthy community and were exempt from paying taxes. The Templars often indicated their tax-free status by placing their emblem of the splayed cross, adopted in 1146, upon many of their houses. There are two eighteenth-century cottages in nearby Whitkirk that display Templar crosses. Many older buildings in Leeds, before demolition and redevelopment took place, displayed such crosses and one can still be seen in the city today on a wall near the river at Lower Briggate. The Thorseby Society (officially the Historical Society for Leeds and District) have recorded that at one time there were nineteen such crosses on buildings in the city – ten alone on Templar Street and at least six on buildings in the Lower Headrow and Lady Lane area. Having a cross on their premises in Leeds gave particular exemption from the 'Leeds Soke'. This permitted owners from having to use the King's Mill in Swinegate to grind corn and therefore presumably exempting them from having to pay tax to the Crown.

The Templars were generally well supported by the monarchy during the twelfth and thirteenth centuries. Richard I, a great Crusader himself, had endorsed their land holdings in the country and given them immunity from pleas and suits. King John had major financial dealings with the Order and Henry III had entrusted some of his financial, diplomatic and military matters to the Templars. Henry also established a chantry in the Temple in London during his reign. Edward I, on his way north to confront the Scots, stopped at Temple Newsam and it is recorded that at least one former Knights Templar Master in Scotland fought on the side of the King at the Battle of Falkirk in 1298. Brian Le Jay died in the battle and has often been considered by many Scots as a traitor to the cause for independence. So reviled was he that it is said that the great Scottish novelist Sir Walter Scott, in his classic medieval story *Ivanhoe*, based his evil Knight Templar character Brian de Bois-Guilbert on that of the turncoat Brian Le Jay. In fact, Scott paints the Knights Templar in a bad light; they are both anti-Islamic and anti-Semitic.

In the novel, the Preceptory of Templestowe is central to the story. There was no preceptory of that name during the Templar period and it has been long thought that Templestowe was based upon Temple Newsam, although a small number of streets in Leeds have this name. Certainly, Scott placed the preceptory in the right area. When Isaac of York visits Templestowe to plead for his daughter Rebecca, the journey is said to be 'but a day's journey'. In reality, the distance between York and Temple Newsam is about 20 miles. Isaac also makes reference to other Jews in Tadcaster, halfway between York and Temple Newsam. The preceptory is described as being set in fair meadows and pastures and would fit well with what we know of the early Temple Newsam preceptory. Templestowe is well fortified, with armed guards at the main entrance, fronted by a drawbridge. Here Scott deviates from fact, for there is no archaeological evidence that Temple Newsam was built in this way. However, given that many Templar establishments were bases for 'warrior-monks' and that Knights Templar would have regularly trained in combat skills, it is not impossible that Temple Newsam had some form of defensive works. Later in the book, before the trial by combat, reference is made to the tolling of the bell in the old church of St Michael's, 'situated in a hamlet at some distance from the preceptory'. This could well have been based upon the church at Whitkirk, which would have been such a hamlet just over a mile from Temple Newsam. Other towns and villages around Temple Newsam are mentioned and Scott surely must have had a model on which to base his Templestowe. What better than that of the real Temple Newsam preceptory?

It was towards the end of the thirteenth century that the Order began to come under pressure. With the defeat of the Templars in 1291 at the Siege of Acre, in the Holy Land, they lost their stronghold in the Kingdom of Jerusalem. They did manage to hold out at another fortress at Tartus for a few more years but when that finally fell in about 1302, their control of the Holy Land had gone. The power of the Order was beginning to wane. Philip IV of France was already in conflict with Pope Boniface VIII over the non-payment of taxes to the Crown by clergy and other matters of allegiance. Phillip was ruthless enough to have a smear campaign levelled at the Pope. Boniface was seized by one of Phillip's agents, and although later rescued, he unfortunately died. The new pope died within a year of taking office and, at Phillip's subtle encouragement, a new French pope was elected, Pope Clement V. A compromise was reached between king and pope but while these ecclesiastical matters appeared to have been settled, Phillip still found himself in debt to the Templars. He was envious of their wealth and, being almost bankrupt himself, saw the Templars as an easy target. To add to his worries, with the loss of the Holy Land they were now without purpose and were a worrying military force; a force that he found potentially threatening. He quickly set about a campaign to discredit the Order and placed William de Nogaret, his chief agent in attacking Pope Boniface, in charge. De Nogaret rapidly drew up a total of 127 accusations against the Order. Barber (1978) breaks these down into seven groups as follows:

The denial of saints, the Virgin Mary and Jesus Christ as Saviour

Idolatry

The denouncement of holy sacraments

The Grand Master hearing confession, even though he was not an ordained priest

Obscene practices at initiations

Misusing donated funds

Secrecy of meetings, the breaking of which was punishable by death.

Phillip struck quickly. Historical legend has it that on Friday, 13 October 1307, all Templar houses in France were raided and members of the Order arrested and subsequently placed on trial. Many Templars were tortured to extract confessions and fifty-four were known to have been burned at the stake for heresy.

While Phillip was actively and harshly persecuting the Templars in France he encouraged his fellow kings in other countries to do the same. In England, King Edward II was not as keen to do so. From one of the earliest records in the Close Court Rolls of Edward II it is clear that Edward acted with a little more benevolence than Phillip:

For certain reasons it is ordained by the King and his council that, on Wednesday next after the feast of the Epiphany, all the brethren of the military order of the Temple in every county of England shall be attached by their bodies by the sheriffs and by certain men of the same counties, and that all their lands and tenements, goods and chattels, ecclesiastical and temporal, shall be taken into the King's hands ... and that the bodies of the Templars shall be guarded in a fitting place elsewhere than in their own places, but not in a hard and vile prison

(20 December 1307)

The Pope had clearly written to Edward upon the matter of the Templars, as indicted by a subsequent record a few days later:

To the Pope. Letter stating that the King fully understands the affairs connected with the Templars, upon which the Pope has written him, and that he will make as speedy execution thereof as possible.

(26 December 1307)

The Templars resident at the Preceptory of Temple Newsam were duly rounded up and sent to be held in York, and their lands were subsequently seized. Whilst Phillip had acted with the utmost speed against the Templars, Edward took a more cautious approach. By 1309, he had allowed the Inquisition to examine those arrested:

To the constable of York castle. Order to receive from Henry de Percy the Templars in his custody, and also from the sheriffs of Northumberland, Cumberland, Westmoreland, Lancaster, Nottingham, and York, whom the King has ordered to lead all the Templars in their custody and in their bailiwicks to York, there to deliver them to the said constable, who is to produce them before the inquisitors appointed by the Pope to inquire concerning the said order.

(14 September 1309)

The Inquisitions carried on into 1310, but the Templars appear to have been treated with a degree of kindness and there is no record of confessions being extracted through torture. Indeed, it seems that in some cases, especially in York, there was a very lax attitude towards confinement:

To the sheriff of York. Order to keep the Templars in his charge in such custody that he can answer for them at the King's order, as the King understands that he permits the Templars whom he lately ordered the sheriffs of Northumberland, Cumberland, Westmoreland, Lancaster, Nottingham, Derby, Salop, and Stafford to send to York castle to be guarded there by the said sheriff to wander about in contempt of the King's order.

(12 March 1310)

The Order of the Knights Templar was officially and finally suppressed by order of Pope Clement at a General Council held in the south of France in April 1312. He had gathered together all the evidence from trials across Europe, not just in France, before presenting his proclamation. It is interesting to note that the Pope used the word 'suppressed' rather than 'condemned'. In doing this there is an indication that the Pope felt there was insufficient evidence to condemn the Order outright. Condemnation would have drawn down upon the Templars much harsher punishments.

In Yorkshire, most of the arrested Templars were pardoned, upon admission of their guilt, and given the opportunity to join the Order of the Knights Hospitalers. Many did so or took an honourable retirement. Many Templar holdings were also passed on to the Knights Hospitalers. The Preceptory of Temple Newsam was one of the few exceptions and was retained by the Crown until it was granted to Sir Robert Holland, who was later beheaded in 1322 for his part in the baronial rebellion against King Edward II. Confiscated once again, the manor of Temple Newsam was then gifted to the King's cousin, Mary, or Marie de St Pol, as she was known. As a teenager she had married the rather elderly Aymer de Valence, the Earl of Pembroke, and so became the Countess of Pembroke. She was widowed in 1324, only three years after her marriage, and remained a widow until her death in 1377. Popular mythology has it that she was 'a maid, wife and widow in one day' (*The Yorkshire Post*, 1926) when her husband had been killed in a jousting tournament on the afternoon of their wedding. However, it is known that he died on 24 June 1324 while on ambassadorial duties in France.

Although Mary had no children, her legacy was that she founded Pembroke College in Cambridge. In 1336, Edward III granted her a manor of Denny in Cambridgeshire, where she founded a Franciscan nunnery in 1342. Because she had no heirs, it was at this time that her lands in Temple Newsam were returned to the Crown and subsequently granted to John d'Arcie, Constable of the Tower of London. It is with the d'Arcie (more commonly spelt Darcy) family that the next chapter of Temple Newsam begins.

Chapter 2

A Troubled and Rebellious House

Lord Darcy, Henry VIII and the Pilgrimage of Grace

The Darcy family were to hold sway over the lands at Temple Newsam for the next two centuries. Sir John Darcy, created the 1st Baron Darcy of Knaith in 1317, became one of the most trusted advisers to Edward III. Born in about 1290 in Knaith in Lincolnshire, his life spanned the reign of three monarchs. He was to hold many important and influential positions throughout his life: High Sherriff of Nottinghamshire, Derbyshire and the Royal Forests; Lord Chief Justice of Ireland; and High Sherriff of both Lancashire and Yorkshire. He was on several occasions a Member of Parliament, Steward to King Edward III and Constable of the Tower of London. He fought at the Battle of Crécy and was one of those entrusted to report the victory to Parliament – quite an illustrious career. It was during his period as the King's Steward in about 1337 that he was granted the lands around Temple Newsam and Temple Hirst, and in 1345 he was granted the rights of 'free warren' across those lands. This exempted the holder from any punishment in hunting game, which was ultimately the property of the sovereign. It also required the holder to maintain and protect the game from others who wished to hunt it. Temple Newsam was only one tract of land owned by John Darcy. He held many acres stretching from Nottinghamshire through to Lancashire.

That there was a habitable building on the site of Temple Newsam is indicated by the fact that Sir John's grandson, another John Darcy, the 3rd Baron Darcy, is recorded as being born at Temple Newsam in 1350. This may not have been a permanent residence for the Darcy family, as other children of that generation were also born in Knaith and Temple Hirst. It is not until the end of the fourteenth century that we begin to see successive generations of the family being born at Temple Newsam, so that by this date the estate appears to have become the family 'seat'.

The last significant member of the Darcy family to have been born here was Thomas Darcy. It was he who began the building of the forerunner of the present house in 1518. The house was very different from the one you see today. It is not exactly certain what this grand residence would have looked like but it has been suggested that it would have been a large red-brick house with a central courtyard, following the lines of many major Tudor buildings of the time. R. Fawcett (1972) makes reference to a main entrance through a gateway in the northern section of the house, which leads into the central courtyard. Opposite this in the southern range was a door that led into the house itself. The Great Hall, the main public room of a Tudor house, would have taken up most of the southern range and would have stood the full height of the house. The western range of the house would have been occupied by private apartments, and the eastern range included the Gallery and Chapel Chamber. Near this were possibly a Musicians' Chamber and a Schoolmaster's Chamber. If we include all the service elements of a great house – kitchen, pantry, buttery, larder, brew house and laundry – we can see that Temple Newsam House must have been quite palatial. Nobody knows precisely how large the house may have been, but it would certainly have been of grandeur enough to suit the status of the Darcy family. We can say that it probably did cover an area equivalent to the 'footprint' of the present remodelled house.

Like his ancestor, Thomas Darcy was closely involved with royalty. Under the reign of Henry VII he was indentured to serve the King in 1492 for a period of one year with 1,000 men at his disposal. A few years later, he was taking an active part in making armed incursions into Scotland. In gratitude for his service to the King he was then made Constable of Bamburgh Castle, in Northumberland, and perhaps more importantly, Deputy of Henry the Duke of York, soon to be King Henry VIII. Shortly after the accession, in 1509, Thomas Darcy was installed as a Knight of the Garter and he went on to be a King's Councillor and a Privy Councillor. He was a man of good standing and was well trusted by the young king, especially in military matters. By 1511, he was leading a force of men to aid the French King Ferdinand in his fight against the Moors, although this came to nothing and Sir Thomas returned home and was with the King when he invaded France in 1513. He was clearly a man of substance and presented himself well. After his death a collection of private papers was discovered, amongst which was this tailor's bill from 1513:

> For making a gown of black satin lined with black velvet, 4s; for a doublet of russet damask, 3s. To the broiderer for quilting the same doublet, 6s 8d, &c.: Total, 'xlxjs iiijd [51s 4d]. Payd bey mey lorde at hes depeyng [departing] fourth of London ljs iiijd, and than all thynges . chlere. Be me Frances Howllson'.
>
> (J. Ridley, 1984)

It was a period when dressing to impress was important for image and status, especially for those around the King. This must have been so for Sir Thomas because he was on the King's list of courtiers to attend with him at the event in 1520 (W. Jerdan, 1842). Arranged by Cardinal Wolsey, this has become known as the 'Field of the Cloth of Gold'. Held in Balinghem, within the English controlled area of Calais, it was an extravagant meeting between King Henry VIII of England and King Francis I of France. A 1545 oil painting in the Royal Collection with the title *The Field of the Cloth of Gold*, attributed to Hans Holbein the Younger, gives us a flavour of just how magnificent the occasion must have been. An Anglo-French treaty had been agreed after the English invasion of France a few years earlier and this meeting was intended to strengthen the bonds of friendship between the two countries, and to underline the international non–aggression pact that Wolsey had brokered previously. Ultimately, how effective the meeting actually was is very much open to conjecture, but Sir Thomas Darcy had the privilege of being there and it always feels impressive to me, as I look at Temple Newsam House today, that this was one of the homes of a person who lived at that time and was involved in such a glorious event. History is never far beneath the surface if we take the time to look.

Sir Thomas Darcy was good friends with Cardinal Wolsey, but friendships can turn sour. Almost immediately after his accession in 1509, Henry VIII had married Catherine of Aragon, the widow of his elder brother Arthur. She was twenty-three and he was barely eighteen years old. On Sunday, 24 June they were crowned together, and this is another event that Darcy would have witnessed. Catherine was a well-liked queen but her life was to be filled with personal tragedy. Her first pregnancy ended in a stillbirth. Her second produced a son, much to Henry's delight, but within two months he died suddenly. There was a further infant death and another stillbirth before Mary was born in 1516. Although the couple tried again for a son, it was not to be. Catherine's final pregnancy produced another girl, who died within a very short time. Mary was to be the only child of Catherine to live to adulthood.

It was this lack of a male heir that began the problems – for Henry, Wolsey, and ultimately, Darcy. Henry felt that after seventeen years of marriage, Catherine was never going to give him the male child that he wanted. Like many monarchs, he had mistresses, and one of the sisters of a particular mistress caught his attention. She was Ann Boleyn and was also one of the ladies in waiting upon Catherine. Henry was spending more time with Anne than with his wife, and the relationship was becoming common knowledge and not fully popular amongst the people. As it was impossible under existing ecclesiastical law for him to divorce Catherine, the King sought for a way to have his marriage annulled. He searched the bible and found in the Book of Leviticus reference that a man should not take his brother's wife as his own, and based his plea to the Pope for annulment of the marriage in that the papal dispensation for him to marry Catherine in the first instance was invalid. Catherine countered this by stating that, as she and Arthur had been children when they were married, the marriage had never been consummated. Therefore, they had not been technically married and she had been a virgin at the time of her marriage to Henry. The political and legal wrangling continued for six years. Cardinal Wolsey was charged with persuading the Pope to grant Henry the annulment he desired so that he could marry Anne, and hopefully produce a male heir to the throne. The debates dragged on for so long that it is suggested that Anne Boleyn and her supporters persuaded Henry that Wolsey was deliberately dragging his heels in the matter. Whether this was true or not, Wolsey was removed from High Office in 1529, although he was allowed to remain as Archbishop of York.

Now, as Sir Thomas Darcy and Wolsey had been good friends for many years, one might expect him to have spoken out in Wolsey's defence, but not so. A petition was sent to the King expressing concern at the situation where spiritual men sit in judgement on temporal men:

We submit that spiritual men are not mete to govern us. … According to the law, spiritual men should not sit upon murders or felonies. They cannot repress seditions or rebellions, nor see to invasions of Scotland, or the defences of the kingdom, and, as great clerks do report, there is no manner of state within this your realm that hath more need of reformation, one to be put under good governments, than the spiritual men. … For surely they and other spiritual men be sore moved against all temporal men.

(J. Ridley, 1984)

Although not specifically mentioning Wolsey, the finger was beginning to be pointed at him. Darcy, under instruction, then drew up a long list of accusations against his old friend, including that of treason. In December 1529, he was one of the signatories on the Articles against Wolsey prepared in Parliament. At that time, Wolsey was on his way to York, and while at Cawood, was arrested and ordered to return to London to face the charges. Sadly, on the return journey he died in Leicester, never having had the opportunity to defend himself.

Wolsey had fallen, and whilst Darcy supported the King as a man throughout the matter, he was unsure about the religious side of affairs. He drew attention to himself in 1532, when, in a response to the Duke of Norfolk's speech declaring that the King had been ill-used by the Pope and that there should be no interference from abroad, he stated that he and his estate were always at the King's disposal but that he understood matrimonial matters to be of a spiritual nature and therefore under ecclesiastical jurisdiction. Several other peers echoed this sentiment, and it is hardly surprising that he was informed that his presence at the Session beginning in 1534 was no longer required. He had been away in London from his Temple Newsam estate since 1529; he was tired and in some physical discomfort and now wanted to return to Yorkshire. He petitioned the King in 1534 from his London home in Mortlake:

I have, by my son Sir Arthur Darcy, 'for whom Almighty God reward your Grace', sent a petition which I beg you to consider. I have lain here and nigh London since the beginning of Parliament continually to my great cost; for, as Mr Butts and Mr Bartlott and many other physicians and surgeons know, I could not, with my infirmities and diseases, go home and return every time of Parliament. In consideration of my age, services, and diseases, 'whereof my rupture came in your service', I beg I may have your pardon under your great seal 'and of the Order of the Garter' to be absent from your high courts of Parliament, St George's feasts, commissions, &c., as my said son will show. Both in my said petition and pardons to take my ease in my poor cabins [his Yorkshire estates], I trust to have your favour, and if your Grace have business in person I trust yet in my litter [letter] to do you service.

(J. Ridley, 1984)

Official authority to absent himself from London was not actually given until late in 1534, the same year as his second son, Arthur, was made Governor of the island of Jersey.

Returning to his Yorkshire estates in about 1535, Darcy was a troubled man. He had given good service for many years to the King and had been a steadfast supporter of the monarchy throughout, but the current state of the nation was giving him cause to doubt. For many in the north of England they may as well have been as remote from the seat of government in London as they were from the moon. They had little time for the political and religious machinations of the King and remained largely Catholic. Theirs was very much a hand-to-hand existence and they looked to the Church for support. When Henry had begun the process of suppressing the monasteries a few years earlier in 1525, it brought about feelings of unrest. Now that the King had succeeded in having his marriage to Catherine, a popular queen in the Catholic north, annulled by Thomas Cranmer, and had gone on to marry Anne Boleyn, these feelings bubbled into resentment. When Henry declared himself as head of the Church in England in 1535, open rebellion was fermenting. It was becoming a dangerous time, and against this background Darcy began secret negotiations with the French Imperial Ambassador and Lord Hussey to invite the French emperor to invade England and put an end to the tyranny. The Wars of the Roses were still within memory and Darcy wished to avoid another open civil war. Whether he requested to return to the north to further develop these plans is not known but he would have been fully aware of the general feelings of unrest in that part of the country. The First Act of Dissolution, in 1536, ordered the closure of many Catholic monasteries and other religious houses. Buildings were destroyed and property looted by the Crown. This was the major cause of the great rebellion, beginning in Lincolnshire and Yorkshire in the October of that year, now known as the Pilgrimage of Grace.

The rebellion was led by a little-known man, Robert Aske. A lawyer by profession, he had been captured by the rebels, and listening to their arguments, was persuaded to join them and use his skills as a lawyer in their cause. He wrote letters outlining the rebels' complaints, insisting that their argument was with the government of the country, not with the King or nobility. He firmly believed that the King had supreme authority:

> Robert Aske never wavered in his belief that a just and well-ordered society was based upon a due recognition of rank and privilege, starting with that of their anointed prince, Henry VIII.
>
> (A.L. Morton, 1938)

Aske was a charismatic leader and a skilled public speaker. He deliberately chose to use the word 'pilgrimage' to underpin the rebellion, to give it a religious basis. He wanted the King to stop the attacks on the Church and the destruction of the monasteries, and to return England to the old Catholic order. Aske asked the insurgents to take an oath to join:

> our Pilgrimage of Grace for the commonwealth … the maintenance of God's Faith and Church militant, preservation of the King's person and issue, and purifying of the nobility of all villein's blood and evil counsellors, to the restitution of Christ's Church and suppression of heretics' opinions.
>
> (J. Ridley, 1984)

Wearing a badge of the Five Wounds of Christ, he led an army of some several thousand men and seized York on 16 October 1536. The King was alarmed at this and wrote to Darcy, whom he still trusted as his supporter in the north, although he was a little surprised at his inactivity in the matter:

This day arrived one Leonard Beckwith with letters to us from the mayor and city of York, and also from Sir George Lawson, showing that the commons [the people] of Beverley, Cottingham, Holdenshire, Marshland, Richmondshire, &c. have assembled to enter the city of York, and attempt things contrary to their allegiance. We wonder you have not advertised us more certainly thereof, nor done your best at the beginning, as we understand you might easily have done for the repression of the same. You shall immediately send your son Sir Arthur with 1,000 persons, who are said to be already assembled in Pomfret [Pontefract], to the said city of York, and do your utmost for its defence, remaining still at Pomfret Castle for its security. Furthermore, you shall follow the directions of the Earl of Shrewsbury, whom we send as our lieutenant general into those parts for the repression of the rebels. You shall declare this to the rest of the gentlemen with you.

(Henry VIII to Darcy, 17 October 1536)

Matters were beginning to move very fast. Darcy remained in Pontefract Castle and on the same day that Henry wrote to him he sent this message to the King:

The insurrection has so increased all over the North that we are in great danger of our lives and see no way how it can be repressed.

(Darcy to Henry VIII, 17 October 1536)

It is possible that the King's letters did not get through to Darcy because the Duke of Suffolk later wrote that the castle was so surrounded by the rebels that this was the case.

By 20 October, the rebels were outside Pontefract Castle. The Archbishop of York had managed to evade capture at the taking of York and had sought shelter with Darcy. However, claiming that he was short of supplies and men, he surrendered the castle to Aske and his followers. This was a major coup for the rebels, and Darcy, the Archbishop and other gentry were compelled to take the oath to join the pilgrimage. For Darcy this was no great hardship as he had been a secret supporter from the beginning, as had the Archbishop.

The rebellion was now in full flood. Aske and his followers held a swathe of land that stretched from Newcastle in the far north into Yorkshire and Lincolnshire. At the mouth of the river Humber, the city of Hull had been fortified and supplied with cannon. The King sent the Duke of Norfolk to meet the rebels at Doncaster and the Earl of Shrewsbury was to support him. They were heavily outnumbered, as Shrewsbury writes:

> This day I received the King's letters commanding me, with haste, to turn my face to the repression of the traitors assembled in Yorkshire ... it appears that the rebels number 40,000 and daily increase, while I and those with me, who intend to advance thither tomorrow are little over 7,000; I beg you will march towards Doncaster and we will do the best we can, either to set some stay, or keep them in play till you come.
>
> (Shrewsbury to Norfolk, 17 October 1536)

The rebels arrived in Doncaster and the Mayor and elders of the town all readily swore the oath to the pilgrimage. Henry faced a dilemma. He could order Norfolk and Shrewsbury to engage the rebels in military action but this could precipitate England into another bloody civil war. Fortunately for Henry, Aske did not want armed conflict but a negotiated peace based on the King's acceptance of their grievances. Accordingly he met with Norfolk in Doncaster and, to avoid the conflict, Norfolk offered to take Aske's requests to the King if he would withdraw his forces. Aske agreed and there was a pause in the rebellion to await Henry's response. But where was Darcy in all of this? He held the castle for the rebels and had developed a close friendship with Robert Aske, with whom he sympathised. But his friendship with the rebel leader had not gone unnoticed. A letter to Thomas Cromwell made the comment that 'His Majesty ... has no great trust in Darcy'.

At the end of October Henry issued these instructions:

> Instructions to the Duke of Norfolk and Sir Will. Fitzwilliam, Lord Admiral, whom the King sends to the North.
>
> Whereas the rebels lately assembled in Yorkshire signified to Norfolk and the Earl of Shrewsbury in a conference at Doncaster that their insurrection had grown upon certain causes which they called abuses,

but that they would withdraw to their houses if Norfolk would signify
their griefs to the King, and take with him Sir Ralph Ellerker and Robert
Bowes to declare them; His Highness having accordingly heard their
complaints and preferring to make a gracious answer, desires the Duke
and Fitzwilliam to repair to Doncaster with a copy of these instructions,
a safeconduct under the Great Seal, a proclamation implying a pardon,
copies of the same, certain books of His Highness' answer, &c.; and
there to act as follows:—

1. On their arrival at Doncaster, being assured by secret espial of
the state of the country, they shall send to Lord Darcy and others to
meet them there with a company not exceeding 300 to hear the King's
answer assuring them of safe passage and re-passage. And if Darcy and
his complices [accomplices] nevertheless refuse to commit themselves
on surety of the Duke's word, they shall declare to them that though
the King would rather have avoided giving them his safeconduct in
his own realm, yet, to avoid extremities, he has agreed to do so, and
the Duke and Admiral shall accordingly send it under his Great Seal.
On their coming they shall first tell them in the King's name that His
Majesty takes their proceedings very unkindly, first, for attempting
rebellion when none of them sued to him for redress of the things they
considered abuses;

   2nd, that although the King might have been justified in repressing
the rebellion with extreme severity, they are so little grateful for his
mercy that he is almost compelled to send his said counsellors to those
parts and put many others to trouble and expense;

   3rd, that, notwithstanding they promised at Doncaster that nothing
should be innovated, they have attempted many unlawful assemblies, the
spoil of many of his subjects, the fortification of Hull and other places,
the firing of beacons, the ringing of their bells awkward, the making
of proclamations, the keeping of the Earl of Cumberland in his castle,
detaining the King's revenues, intercepting his letters, &c. The Duke
and Lord Admiral shall therewith make unto them, as it were, a friendly
exhortation, showing what great cause they have on their knees to thank
God that hath sent them so merciful a prince, and how far their doings

have varied from their pretence. For first their pretence was to maintain the Faith, and what is more contrary to God's Commandment than rebellion? Then they said they made their insurrection for the common wealth, and have they not injured many and robbed many honest and poor men? Is it a common wealth for poor men to leave their lands untilled, their corn unsown, to leave their wives and children, to rise like madmen against their Prince? The Duke and Admiral shall enforce the subject to the best of their wisdom, and reproach them with having set up a traitorous villain as their governor who writes himself so as he says by the consent of the baronage of those parts. If Lord Darcy and others with him persist in their malice and demand an answer to their articles, the Duke and Admiral shall reply that although their articles were in such general form that certain answer could not be conveniently made to them, yet His Majesty, as a merciful prince, has put his own pen to the answering of every article in a much more certain sort than the articles were proponed [sic], so that all indifferent men must be contented. Nevertheless they are commanded to stay the publication of the same till they perceive conformity in the rest, or else inform His Majesty of their obstinacy. If on this Darcy and the others desire the King's pardon without further conditions, they shall first show some of them secretly the said proclamation of pardon, to the intent they may assist in the apprehension of those vile persons that are excepted. Then they shall deliver to them copies of His Grace's answer, and cause the proclamation to be openly published. If the men submit they shall cause those present to receive such oaths as the Lincolnshire men have sworn, and further promise to do anything required for the King's honour and declaration of their repentance. When the oath is administered to Darcy and the other principal persons they shall insist on the miseries that ensue of such insurrections, and command them to have vigilant regard to apprehend seditious persons who spread tales. Leaves much to their discretion, but if the rebels refuse to submit they shall first advertise the King with all diligence, and meanwhile advise them by way of private counsel, to weigh the dangers of their obstinacy, that by staying them from any new attempts the King may meanwhile make his preparations against them while they are unprovided [sic], and thus having gained five or six days,

immediately to make proclamation that all who wish to be taken for true
subjects shall forbear from making any new insurrection, and treat those
as traitors who would move them thereto.

(Henry VIII letters, October 1536)

It appeared for the moment that the rebels had won. The King had shied
away from military action and, on the surface, seemed to be taking their
demands seriously. He was offering a safe passage to Doncaster and a promise
of a pardon to the leaders if they abstained from further insurrection and
swore an oath of allegiance to the King. I think it is significant that Darcy is
referred to by name many times in the document, as if he was the leader of
the rebellion. Aske gets no mention whatsoever and is presumably bracketed
within the terms 'others', 'complices' and 'other principle persons'. It is
quite clear from the wording of the document that Henry considers Darcy
to be one of the rebel leaders, if not *the* rebel leader. However, in early
December, Darcy and the others received their pardons and they dispersed.
The rebel gentry gathered together at Pontefract Castle in early December
and drew up the '24 Articles' in a petition to the King. These were presented
to Norfolk on 6 December, and the rebels were promised:

The King would receive their demands.
A freely elected parliament would be held in York to discuss them.
All pilgrims were to be pardoned for their part in the rebellion.

Aske was so overjoyed that he made this written proclamation:

Loving neighbours, the King by mouth has declared to me that
the pardon granted at Doncaster shall extend to all, and that your
reasonable petitions shall be ordered by Parliament. His Grace, for the
love he bears to this country, intends to keep Parliament at York and
have the Queen crowned there. His Grace esteems the commonwealth
of the realm and the love of his subjects more than any other earthly
riches and will send down the Duke of Norfolk to minister justice till
his coming.

(Aske's Manifesto)

The conflict appeared to be over and everyone seemed to have won; the rebels were to get their grievances heard by the King; Henry had avoided a civil war and nobody had been punished. It was a good result for all. Or was it? In late December, Aske had been invited to London to discuss the submitted Articles with the King. Aske was seduced by Henry's charm but the King was stalling. Whilst appearing friendly and honest, he was in fact using Aske as a source of information on the rebel leaders. Darcy was also summoned to London in the January, but in a lengthy letter he pleaded to be excused through age and infirmity. He also underlined his former service to the King, perhaps wishing to establish his good name in the eyes of the King.

> Never fainted nor feigned in service to the King his father nor him above fifty years, in war nor in peace; but since coming from the lords of the Council last at Doncaster, has not thrice come down from his chamber. Has been so vehemently handled with his two diseases of rupture and flux, as the Lord Admiral, Mr Browen, and Mr Russell saw at Doncaster, and as all the King's physicians know, that he feels more like to die than to live. Would rather die than have the King believe that he should of his own free will, not compelled by lack of all furniture of war, and by extreme fury of the commons, enter into their follies, as, he hears, has been reported. ... Finally, if he have any recovery of health, and have licence to come by sea, which he may do from his house, he will, on the King's command, come up by sea or in a litter, or die by the way.
>
> (Darcy to Henry VIII, 6 January 1537)

He remained in Yorkshire and had been given the surety of Pontefract Castle and had the office of maintaining it in the King's name. However, on 10 February 1537, he wrote to Aske requesting him:

> re-deliver, secretly, to bearer, Darcy's constable, all arrows, bows, and spears he took from the castle.
>
> (Darcy to Aske, 10 February 1537)

Was this to re-arm the castle in the King's name or was it to reinforce his own position in regards of any further rebellion? It could have been either, but a second, short-lived rebellion had broken out in the north-west during January, led by Sir Francis Bigod. Realising that the King was stalling for time, Bigod raised a small force but was not well supported. Aske himself wrote to the rebels questioning their actions when the King had pardoned the north for the rebellion of the previous year and he was persuaded by Henry to command a small force against Bigod and the rebels. Bigod's forces were captured in an attempt to storm the port of Hull and although Bigod escaped, he was taken on 10 February. Was it more than just a coincidence that Darcy should write to Aske on that same day?

The second rebellion gave Henry the excuse he had been looking for. He reneged upon the promises that he had given and in March invited both Aske and Darcy to London, ostensibly to thank them for their part in suppressing Bigod's rebellion. On their arrival they were arrested and placed in the Tower of London. Henry's retribution was swift. He had suppressed two rebellions against him and the leaders were now detained and awaiting trial. Darcy was accused of treason and evidence was brought against him in reports of what he had said. He was reported as being overheard to say that it was better to rule than be ruled, and that if his friend Aske were to be taken by the King he would rescue him if it were to cost 20,000 men's lives. Darcy and the other ringleaders of the rebellion – Aske, Hussey and Constable – were all found guilty of high treason and sentenced to be executed. Aske was hanged, drawn and quartered in York, and Hussey in Lincoln. Constable was hanged in Hull. At first, Henry wanted Darcy to be executed in Doncaster, but it was feared that with his popularity in that region it might instigate a new uprising. Henry relented and Darcy was beheaded on Tower Hill in London on 30 June 1537, and his head then displayed on London Bridge.

After two centuries of controlling the Temple Newsam estates, the Darcy family ended in ignominy. The family was stripped of its lands and the Temple Newsam estate returned to the Crown; it would be several years before the estate would have a new owner. But the crowning legacy of Sir Thomas Darcy's life is surely that he built the first Temple Newsam House, remnants of which can still be found in the present house.

Chapter 3

A Scottish House

Lord Darnley and Mary Queen of Scots

With the suppression of the Pilgrimage of Grace and the execution of its leaders, Temple Newsam – the Yorkshire estate belonging to the Darcy family – had been seized yet again by the Crown, and would remain the property of the King for some years. As the rebellion came to its bloody conclusion one might have expected a period of calm to descend over Henry's England. But this was not to be; there were the Scots still to contend with.

The friction between England and Scotland had been long standing, even though the Scottish king, James IV, had signed a peace treaty with Henry in 1502. In the following year, James had married Henry's sister, Margaret. It was hoped that this would bring more unity between the two nations but James had renewed his alliance with France, causing another war, which ended with James's death on the battlefield of Flodden in 1513. He was succeeded by his infant son, James V, and Scotland was ruled by successive regents until he assumed full power in 1528. Scotland was still a predominantly Catholic country aligned with France and it is hardly surprising that, in 1537, James should take a French wife. His first wife, Madeleine de Valois, the daughter of Francis I of France, was not a healthy young woman and sadly died within a year of the marriage. James went on to marry again – Mary de Guise, another French woman. From this marriage there was one surviving child, Mary, born in 1542 in Linlithgow Palace, Scotland.

When James's mother, sister of Henry VIII, died in 1541, further war broke out between Scotland and England. It was short-lived and ended disastrously for James with the Battle of Solway Moss in October 1542, and he retired to Falkirk Palace. He died there on 15 December, only a matter of days after his daughter Mary was born. She acceded to the throne of Scotland at the age of just six days. Henry now saw an opportunity to align the two nations and in 1543 he proposed a marriage between Mary and his son, Prince Edward. Under the Treaty of Greenwich the marriage would have taken place when Mary was ten years old and she would then move to England, where she would be brought up in the English court.

This would have been a good move for Henry, had it not been for the question of religion. There was a growing Protestant faction within the largely Catholic Scotland. With Mary only an infant, the power balance between contesting regents shifted from one side to the other: Cardinal Beaton, the Catholic, and the Earl of Arran, the Protestant. With Beaton in the ascendency there was a push towards a renewal of the old alliance with France. Although Arran initially objected, he backed down and shortly after Mary's coronation in 1543, he became a Catholic. The Treaty of Greenwich was torn up by the Scottish parliament and the proposed marriage to the English prince was rejected. Henry was furious and set out on a military campaign against the Scots to enforce the marriage. This action became known as the 'Rough Wooing' and continued for several years. Mary was moved from castle to castle to avoid the English forces until, at the age of five, it was agreed with King Henry II of France to send her to the French court. She remained there for several years, until at the age of sixteen she was married to the King's son, Francois. She became Queen of France the following year, when her husband became king, but unfortunately he died after one year. In 1560, at the age of eighteen, Mary was a widow.

The land of her birth was calling and she returned to Scotland in 1561 to become Mary, Queen of Scotland. While she had been growing up in France, England had seen the passing of three monarchs: Henry VIII, Edward VI and Mary I. England was now ruled by a new queen, Elizabeth I. But the Catholic-Protestant struggles were still to continue and Temple Newsam was to play an important part in all of this.

After Mary's father, James IV, died, her mother married Archibald Douglas, the sixth Earl of Arran. The marriage produced a daughter, Margaret Douglas, niece of Henry VIII. At the age of thirteen she was brought from Scotland to be educated with Mary Tudor, later to be Mary I, in London. She was, to all accounts, a beautiful young woman and a rising star at court. She rose to become Lady of Honour to the Princess Elizabeth, later to be Elizabeth I. But she was also wilful and headstrong, and became secretly betrothed to Sir Thomas Howard. For this they were both placed in the Tower of London, although she only spent four months there. The Tower was to be her home on several occasions throughout her life, as we shall see.

Enter Matthew Stewart, the fourth Earl of Lennox. He was a man of personal political ambition and saw little problem in choosing the best side to be on for himself. Although Catholic by birth, he was quite happy to support Henry in his Reformist policies, and with a somewhat tenuous claim to the Scottish throne, he promoted himself in England as the Protestant claimant of the Kingdom of Scotland. His offer of support to the English king came on the condition that he should marry the volatile and strong-willed Margaret. Henry saw this as an ideal opportunity to align the English and Scottish royal families and agreed to the marriage. On 6 July 1544, they were married in St James's Palace in London before Henry and his queen, Catherine Parr. As a dowry, Henry gifted the estates of Temple Newsam to Margaret and she retired there after the marriage, while her husband was sent by Henry to Scotland on military expeditions. Margaret was a staunch Catholic and made no secret of it. Her home at Temple Newsam became a focus for Catholic activities in Yorkshire.

In 1545, the marriage produced a son, Henry Stuart, Lord Darnley, and it is by this name that he is commonly known in history. If you visit Temple Newsam House today you will find a room known as the 'Darnley Room'. Now very much altered from its original state, it has always been referred to as the room in which Lord Darnley was born, although this in fact is unlikely and is very much a construction of a later owner. F.W. Crossley (1918–19) details an inventory of the house taken in 1565 and indicates that the house was furnished and decorated in a splendid style. The Great Hall was hung with a 'tester of cloth of gold and silver with the arms of the Earl and his wife embroidered on it and curtains of crimson damask'. 'Lord Darnley's Chamber' was hung with tapestries of hawking and hunting. One can only imagine the opulence in which the young Darnley grew up.

Darnley's early years were spent in the rural idyll of Temple Newsam and its surroundings. He quickly developed a keen mind and an athletic body. He was schooled in Latin and could speak both French and Scottish. He would also have been taught to dance and play at least one musical instrument, as well as learning how to discourse and write verse. These were requisite of any cultured Renaissance nobleman. Darnley was a good horseman and keen on hunting. One can imagine that much of his training would have been in those years riding on the estate. He was certainly at Temple Newsam in 1554 because he sent a letter from there to Mary I explaining that he would love nothing better than to be a soldier. Beautifully penned in the newly fashionable italic hand, some say dictated by his tutor, it portrays a maturity and eloquence far beyond his young age. A copy of the letter can still be seen today in the British Library and is not difficult to read, as can be seen in this excerpt:

> but I am also enflamed and stirred, even now my tendre aige not withstanding, to be serving Your Grace, wishing every haire in my heade for to be a worthy souldiour, of that same self hert, mynde, and stomake that I am of.

Like his mother, he was a Catholic at heart, but when taken to the court of Elizabeth I as a teenager, he embraced Protestantism as well. He would have been made astutely aware of his social position. Through his mother and grandmother, he was a claimant to the throne of England, and through his father, Matthew Stewart, he also had a claim to the Scottish crown. It is little wonder that his parents felt that he was destined for high office.

Darnley was tall, well over 6 feet, athletic and handsome, with fair hair and grey eyes. He cut a fine figure at court and knew how to wear clothes well and present himself. According to records, he was a witty conversationalist, a fine lute player and a catch for any aspiring young lady at court.

At that time, Queen Elizabeth was acutely aware that the arrival of Mary in Scotland as the new queen presented a potential threat to her own position. Elizabeth had declared England to be a Protestant country, but Mary had always felt that she had a stronger claim to the English throne than did Elizabeth. Through Catholic eyes, Elizabeth was illegitimate, and Mary, as the senior descendant of Henry VIII's elder sister Margaret, had the rightful claim. If Mary were to be Queen of England then Catholicism would be ushered back in and the old religious conflicts would resurface. This was a worry to Elizabeth and her councillors. One way in which she could alleviate the situation was for Mary to marry someone from the English nobility who was a staunch supporter of Elizabeth. A prime candidate was Robert Dudley. He had been a favourite of Elizabeth's for many years and one of her closest advisers. It was even rumoured at one time that he would have married her if the way had been clear. Negotiations with Mary began and although she intimated that she might be interested, Dudley appeared not so keen. To encourage him, Elizabeth even gave him estates in Kenilworth and made him Earl of Leicester, but fate was to take a hand.

Margaret Douglas, now Countess of Lennox, had plans for her son Lord Darnley. She was keen for him to make an impression on Mary and, should a match occur, then that would strengthen his claim on the English throne for himself. She petitioned Elizabeth that Darnley should go to Scotland to visit his father. Elizabeth agreed, and in February 1565, Mary met Darnley at Wemyss Castle. For Mary it was love at first sight and she soon became enamoured of him. They were in fact first cousins and a match between them would strengthen both their claims to both the English and Scottish thrones. Their blatant liaison began to create a stir amongst the Protestant Scottish nobility and in London. In a letter of 7 April 1565, Lord Randolph wrote to London:

> the matter is now grown to further ripeness. The Queen's familiarity with him [Darnley] breeds no small suspicion that there is more intended than merely giving him honour for his nobility. ... It is now commonly said, and I believe is more than a bruit [rumour], that this queen has already such good liking of him, that she can be content to forsake all other offers ... and content herself with her own choice.
>
> (Randolph to Cecil, 1565)

Darnley had been ill with the measles shortly after their first meeting and Mary was so concerned for his health that she was rarely away from his side, even delaying necessary journeys to be with him. This caused even more reaction from her people:

Darnley is not fully recovered, and for that cause the Queen stays her journey to St Johnstons for a few days. Her care has been marvellous great and tender over him. Such tales and bruits [rumours] of her doings spread abroad, that it is wonder to hear the discontent of her people: I speak not of the common sort, whom I trust least, but of the wisest in the realm—and in a word to say it, 'never anye in her govermente worce lyked' [never anyone in her government worse liked].

(Randolph to Cecil, 29 April 1565)

Darnley was clearly making enemies but it was a whirlwind romance with daily tokens of love passing between them. Mary gave Darnley the Bishopric of Ross, creating him Earl of Ross, and his father had also now deferred the title of Earl of Lennox to him. Rumours soon spread that Mary intended to marry Darnley, causing great consternation in Scotland and England. In early June, a meeting of the Privy Council was convened in London to discuss 'the perils to the Queen of England and her realm by this intended marriage of the Queen of Scots and Lord Darnley' and, perhaps more importantly, what should be done about it. The Council considered that the proposed marriage would only strengthen Mary's claim upon the English throne and give encouragement to the 'Romish' religion. Their major piece of advice in countering the effects was for Queen Elizabeth to marry, presumably to produce a legitimate heir to the throne, although this is not stated. They also recommended that the Countess of Lennox, Darnley's mother, be 'secluded from intelligence' and that her son and husband be recalled to London. Failing this, their English estates would be forfeited. Elizabeth wrote to Mary with this request:

For divers good causes we have expressly commanded the Earl of Lennox and his eldest son Henry Lord Darnley, as our subjects, to return hither without delay: and we require you to give them your safe conduct for their speedier coming.

(Elizabeth to Mary, 18 June 1565)

They didn't. In fact, things went from bad to worse for Elizabeth. A few weeks later, in July, she received information that the couple had secretly married:

On Monday last the 9th this queen was secretly married in her own palace to the Lord Darnley, not above seven persons present; 'and wente that daye to their bedde to the Lord Setons howse' [and went that day to their bed in the Lord Seton's house]. This is known by one of the priests present at the mass. If true, Your Majesty sees how her promise is kept, and may measure the rest of her doings.

(Randolph to Elizabeth, 16 July 1565)

The marriage was officially declared on 29 July in Holyrood Palace, in Edinburgh. Darnley, of Temple Newsam, was now King Consort of Scotland, just one small step away from being a de facto king. His mother should have been overjoyed, and she probably was. Her objective had been realised – to put her son in a powerful position and to secure his claim on the throne – but it was to her cost. As recommended by the Privy Council, she was arrested and sent to the Tower of London. Lennox's estates in England, including Temple Newsam, were attainted and duly seized by the Crown. Elizabeth became acrimonious towards Mary. She instructed one of her Private Chamber, John Thomworth (sometimes Tamworth), to make her feelings clear to the Queen. She voiced her displeasure at the marriage and demanded to know why Mary had married Darnley without her royal consent. She reissued her demand that Lennox and Darnley (she would not deign to refer to him as either Mary's husband or King) be returned to England. Elizabeth even used emotional blackmail against them, advising them to remember that the Lady Margaret was in the Tower and her well-being depended upon their actions. She accused Lennox of duplicity in first going to Scotland on the pretence of visiting his estates and then getting his son to join him there with the purpose of marrying him to Mary.

Mary countered by informing Elizabeth that she had married Darnley in all good sincerity and that she had offered to defer consummation of the marriage for a short period while any doubts that Elizabeth should have over the marriage be resolved by commissioners from both countries. She also claimed that Elizabeth had openly refused this offer and therefore Mary saw no reason not to proceed with her plans. As for retaining Lennox and her husband in Scotland, she saw no reason why they should not remain there, as one was an earl of Scotland and the other her husband! Elizabeth did not take this reply well. When the Scottish ambassador went to see her with a letter from Lennox to his wife Margaret in the Tower, she refused to receive it. Elizabeth made it clear that she considered both Lennox and Darnley to be traitors. But whereas Elizabeth was displeased with the marriage, the response from other monarchs was quite different. The King of Spain wrote to his ambassador, Guzman de Silva, on 6 June 1565:

> I note from your letters ... the information he gave you respecting the state of the match of the Queen of Scotland with Lord Darnley, son of Lady Margaret, and also the intelligence you obtained from Lady Margaret herself, and from the Earl of Leicester to the effect that the marriage had taken place. Your news on this head has been very pleasing to me, and, on the presumption that the marriage of the Queen and Darnley has really gone so far, the bridegroom and his parents being good Catholics and our affectionate servitors; and, considering the Queen's good claims to the crown of England, to which Darnley also pretends, we have arrived at the conclusion that the marriage is one that is favourable to our interests and should be forwarded and supported to the full extent of our power.
>
> You may, however, convey to Lady Margaret Lennox the sympathy and goodwill I bear towards her son, and the successful accomplishment of the project, in order that they may be satisfied and may know that they can depend upon me in matters concerning this business, and so be able to entertain and encourage the Catholics and their party in England
>
> You will make Lady Margaret understand this, and that not only shall I be glad for her son to be King of Scotland and will help him thereto, but also to be King of England if this marriage is carried through.
>
> (King of Spain to Guzman de Silva, 1565)

Even as first cousins, Mary and Darnley needed a dispensation from the Pope, which he had no hesitation in granting:

> The Pope announced that the Queen of Scotland had chosen for husband an Englishman, her near kinsman, and therefore craved a dispensation.

Of the behaviour and disposition of this noble he heard nothing that was not admirable; but the Queen of England had endeavoured to hinder the match. The nobleman, however, had escaped from England, and gave out that he was next in succession to the throne of England upon the Queen's death. The Queen of Scotland and her [intended] husband promised to defend the Catholic faith. The Pope therefore saw no reason why he should not with all speed release and dispense them from the laws. ... And so, lest religion should be jeopardized in that country, he had resolved to grant this dispensation.

(St Mark's Rome, 1 September 1565)

So it would seem that only Elizabeth and her Protestant supporters in Scotland stood against the marriage. Some Scottish nobles raised an army against Mary, but these were quickly beaten in a short but bloody battle and the way was clear for Mary and Darnley. He was king in name only and he wanted to share the matrimonial crown in full right, but for some reason Mary hesitated and would not agree.

For all his good looks and charm, Darnley was not the most pleasant of men. He drank, womanised and generally lived the good life. He was also outrageously jealous, and had a quick temper. From his early days in Scotland he was described as having an intolerable pride and arrogance. He was full of boasting and said to be swift to come to blows, and there was an immense hatred towards him.

By 1566, Mary was pregnant with their first child, but with Darnley following a debauched life and often leaving her alone, it was little wonder that she began to rely upon her Private Secretary, David Rizzio (sometimes Riccio). That they spent much time in each other's company is not disputed but there is little evidence that he may have been the father of the child she was carrying. Darnley believed otherwise and was consumed with jealousy. This was noticed in February 1565 by Lord Randolph:

The suspicion of this Kynge towardes David [Rizzio] is so greate that it muste shortlye growe to a scabbe amonge them [The suspicion of this King towards David is so great that it must shortly come to a head].

(Randolph to Cecil, 25 February 1566)

It did come to a head on 9 March. Darnley, encouraged by some other Protestant nobles, plotted to dispose of Rizzio. Chief amongst the plotters was Lord Ruthven, who also seemed to have a personal grudge against Rizzio. In the evening, Mary – now at least six months' pregnant – was in her private chamber with Rizzio and some ladies in waiting. They had been playing cards, a popular pastime, and listening to Rizzio playing the lute. Darnley and his conspirators burst into the room. Fearing for her own life, Mary ordered them from the room but a loaded pistol was held against her while Rizzio was pulled from behind the Queen and stabbed fifty-six times. His body was then dragged out and thrown down the stairs, where it was stripped of its valuables by servants. Within two hours, the body was disposed of in Holyrood Palace cemetery, although Mary later ordered it to be exhumed and placed in the sepulchre of the kings of Scotland – an action that raised many eyebrows. Darnley's dagger was left in the body after the murder but it has never been proved that he actually struck the blow. Some say that his dagger was taken from him, as he refused to strike Rizzio, and used by one of the murderers; others say that he struck the first blow. However, in a letter to Cecil on 21 March, Randolph claims that Darnley stated that the murder was by his command and that he had given him one blow himself, and that to show that the deed was his, the dagger had been left in the body. Whatever the truth of the matter, this action was the beginning of Darnley's downfall and the Queen never forgave him. It was to have grave consequences. Darnley did relent after the attempted coup and helped Mary escape to Dunbar, but a few weeks later she returned to Edinburgh. The Earl of Bothwell provided her with an armed force and her would-be attackers fled into exile.

On 19 June 1566, Mary gave birth to a son, christened a few months later as Charles James. This child was the heir apparent and would later become James VI of Scotland and, ultimately, James I of England. After the birth Mary ensured that Darnley publicly acknowledged the child as his to counter the ongoing rumours that Rizzio may have been the father. Some Protestant nobles suggested that Rizzio was in reality a Papist spy sent to infiltrate the court and support Mary against these nobles. Although Darnley did acknowledge his son, he refused to attend the Catholic christening at Stirling Castle later in December, preferring to be elsewhere carousing.

Before the christening, Mary had been unwell and had been at Craigmillar Castle, just outside of Edinburgh, to recuperate. While there she had been meeting with her advisers. Her husband was becoming a serious problem to both her and her country. Her earlier infatuation of him had now turned sour and he was proving to be a thoroughly unlovable man. She could not divorce him under Catholic law and an annulment of the marriage would make her son illegitimate and therefore unable to succeed her to the throne. They discussed the available alternatives, one of which was that the problem would be solved should he conveniently die. The nobles continued their discussions well into the night and reputedly signed the 'Craigmillar Bond' – an agreement to remove Darnley. There is no copy of this bond and it is still uncertain as to whether Mary herself was party to this agreement.

Early in February 1567, Darnley was lying ill in Glasgow. It has been suggested, and highly probable given his debauched lifestyle, that he was suffering from syphilis. Mary travelled to see him. Whether this was out of genuine concern or with a more sinister motive is not known. Darnley, with all the charm he could muster, tried to seduce Mary into letting him return to her. His words were recorded by one Thomas Crawford, who was present at their meeting and overheard their conversation, as he later officially declared. Darnley's words read like an extract from a soap opera of today:

The words that I remember betwixt the King and Queen in Glasco [Glasgow] when she took him away to Edinburgh:—

When they met, she asked him of his letters complaining of the cruelty of 'som'. … He said in reply to her, she was the cause of his sickness, and 'Ye asked me what I ment by the crueltye specified in my lettres? yt procedethe of you onelye that wille not accepte mye offres and repentance. I confesse that I have failed in som thinges, and yet greater faultes have bin made to you sundrye times, which ye have forgiven. I am but yonge, and ye will saye ye have forgiven me diverse tymes. Maye not a man of mye aege for lacke of counselle, of which I am verye destitute, falle twise or thrise, and yet repent and be chastised by experience? Yf I have made anye faile, that ye but thinke a faile, howe so ever it be, I crave your perdone and proteste that I shall never faile againe. I desire no other thinge but that we maye be togeather as husband and wife. And if ye will not consent hereto, I desire never to rise forth of thys bed. Therefore I praye you give me an aunswer hereunto. God knowethe howe I ame punished for makinge my God of you, and for having no other thowght but on you. And if at anie tyme I offend you, ye are the cause, for that when anie offendethe me, if for mye refuge I might open mye minde to you, I woulde speake to no other, but when anie thinge ys spoken to me, and ye and I not beinge as husband and wife owght to be, necessite compellethe me to kepe it in my breste and bringethe me in suche melancolye as ye see me in.'

It may have been perfectly possible that Darnley, riddled with syphilis, had genuinely seen the errors of his ways and wanted them to return to a life of married bliss. It is equally possible that he realised he would perhaps be safer to be reunited with her. To be seen back in the position of King Consort with Mary might just offer him some protection against his enemies. I am sure he was not so arrogant as to not be aware of his decidedly uncertain position. In response to his pleas, Mary did not openly pardon him but hinted that she would take him back, but on condition:

She was very 'pensiffe' [thoughful], and he found fault; and said he heard she had brought a litter with her. She said it was brought to carry him more softly than on horseback. He said a sick man should not so travel, 'in so colde weather' [in such cold weather]. She answered she would take him to Craigmiller to be with him 'and not farre from her sonne' [and not far from her son].

He said he would go, if they might be at bed and board as husband and wife, and she to leave him no more: and if she promised this on her word, he would go where she pleased – without this, he would not go. She said if she had not been so minded, she would not have come so far, and gave him her hand and faith of her body, that she would love and use him as her husband. But before they could come together, 'he must be purged and clensed of hys sicknesse [purged and cleansed of his sickness] ... for she minded to give him the bathe at Craigmiller.'

It is interesting to note that Mary talked of Darnley being 'purged' of his illness and that she wanted to 'give him the bathe'. During the sixteenth century, syphilis had reached almost epidemic proportions and one of the favoured remedies was to take a 'sweat bath' to induce sweating and salivation. This was thought to rid the body of syphilitic toxins. Is this a further indication that Darnley was suffering from syphilis?

Darnley did return with Mary, although not to Craigmillar Castle, as he considered it too cold and draughty in his condition. He would much rather have returned to Holyrood Palace but was persuaded to lodge in a house known as Kirk O'Field, a short distance away, near the church. Did Mary want to keep her sick husband away from her young son for fear of contagion or could there have been another reason? Whichever it was, Mary visited Darnley at the house on the night of 9 February before returning to the palace. During the early hours of the next morning, the peace was shattered by an enormous explosion. People rushed out to find that there was barely anything left of the house in which Darnley had been lodging. Enough gunpowder had been placed beneath the house to completely destroy it. Darnley was found dead in a garden a little distance from the house. He was dressed in his nightgown and there were no obvious signs that he had been caught in an explosion. Indeed, it was commented that he looked as if he had been strangled. With him were two servants, also dead. Near the bodies was found a length of rope and a chair. Had Darnley been awoken and attempted to escape and then was strangled in the garden? Why was there one solitary undamaged chair there? A report sent by Seigneur de Clarnault the following week gives quite a clear unbiased account of what happened:

That on Sunday the 9th about 7.00 pm the Queen with the principal nobles at Court visited the King – stayed two or three hours, and then attended the marriage of one of her gentlemen, as she had promised; or it is thought she would have staid till midnight or 1.00 am, seeing their good agreement for three weeks past. She retired soon from the 'nopce' [nuptials], to go to bed. And about 2.00 am a tremendous noise was heard, as if a volley of twenty-five or thirty cannon, arousing the whole town; and on her sending to know whence it came, they found the King's 'logis' [lodgings] totally destroyed, and himself sixty or eighty 'pas' [paces] from the house in a garden, dead, also his valet de chambre and a young page. One may imagine the distress and agony of this poor princess, such a misfortune chancing when Her Majesty and the King were on such good terms. It is well seen this unhappy affair proceeded from an underground mine: as yet the author is unknown.

(Report of M. de Clarnault, 16 February 1567)

Were the King and Queen on such good terms? Although Clarnault is correct in that nobody knew who was responsible for the explosion, rumours were rife. Some said that Mary herself was complicit in the act; others that the act was committed by the Earl of Bothwell, whom Mary later married in May of that year. Eyewitness accounts from people living near the house that was destroyed all spoke of seeing or speaking to men coming *from* the scene and moving towards the town. Barbara Mertine swore that just before the explosion occurred she was at her window and heard thirteen men coming from the area, passing into Cowgate and up Friars Wynd [alleyway]. As the explosion happened she saw eleven men coming from the Friars Yett [gateway], the area where the house was. She called out to them as they passed, accusing them of being traitors. Another woman, May Crokat, had been in bed with her twins at the time of the explosion. It was so loud that she feared it came from the house above, and she ran to the door. As she did so she saw eleven men coming from the Friars Yett. One she recognised by his silks, and she asked where the explosion was. They did not reply. Seven hurried away down Cowgate and the other four up the Wynd [Friars Wynd].

From both testimonies it is clear that a large group of men were somehow involved in the event. Whoever had been responsible, it remained that Darnley was now dead at the age of twenty-two. Mary's problem had been solved. Bothwell was arrested in April and tried for the murder but he was acquitted through lack of conclusive evidence. Mary's popularity, what remained of it after her marriage to Darnley, was fast waning in the eyes of the people. After Bosworth and Mary married, there was an uprising against them and Mary was forced to abdicate in favour of her son, James. She fled to England, where she threw herself on the mercy of Elizabeth, who, still considering her a threat to her own position, had her imprisoned in various castles for the next eighteen years. After being found guilty of plotting to assassinate Elizabeth, she was beheaded on 8 February 1587.

From his early years in Temple Newsam, Darnley's mother had always had high ambitions for her son. She had engineered his marriage to Mary, and Darnley had risen to the position of King Consort to a queen. She had hoped that this would strengthen his claim to the throne of England. Elizabeth had despised them both and it is somewhat ironic that their son, James VI of Scotland, should be invited to be James I of England. In a way, the Countess of Lennox had achieved her ambitions, but the name of Darnley lives on through history as one of the most puzzling unsolved murder mysteries of the seventeenth century.

Chapter 4

A Dynastic House

Sir Arthur Ingram and a house divided

In March 1603, Queen Elizabeth I died, ending 118 years of Tudor reign in England. She was succeeded by James VI of Scotland, a Stuart, who was now to become James I of England. He had been King of Scotland since the age of one, when his mother, Mary Queen of Scots, had been forced to abdicate, shortly after the murder of his father, Lord Darnley. Until he took full control in 1581, Scotland had been managed by a succession of regents. The English court hoped for a breath of fresh air; gone was the old Tudor regime and a new Stuart reign was ushered in, with all the hopes for a settlement of the aged conflict between England and Scotland. When James arrived in London in May 1603, he was welcomed by cheering crowds. Although the two nations were to remain independent sovereign states with their own parliaments and laws, James now ruled in personal union as King of Scotland, England and Ireland.

It was also hoped that this union between the nations under one monarch would bring amity between the two religions. James, born a Catholic, readily embraced Protestantism but he tolerated crypto-Catholicism, knowing that he would have need of the support of the Catholic nobility at court. The infamous and unsuccessful Gunpowder Plot of 1605, a Catholic conspiracy to blow up the Houses of Parliament at the State Opening on 5 November, did bring about an anti-Catholic backlash, with the subsequent passing of the Popish Recusants Act the following year. This barred Catholics from practising the law or medicine and required anyone, on demand, to make an oath of allegiance and deny the Pope's authority over the monarchy of England. In spite of this, James continued to tolerate Catholicism whilst at the same time attempting to bring about some conformity to the Protestant clergy. James's greatest legacy in this field was perhaps in the commissioning of a new translation of the Bible that resolved the many discrepancies in the various differing translations in existence at the time. This resulted in the Authorised King James version of the Bible, still widely used today.

James had many 'favourites' within his courtly circle. Amongst these was a young man called Ludovick Stuart, who at the age of nine took the title 2nd Duke of Lennox after the death of his father in 1583. Ludovick was distant cousin through James's grandfather, James II of Scotland. James the VI of Scotland, as he was then, was very fond of Ludovick, and gave instructions for the boy to remain within the King's household and receive an education there. He lavished titles and estates upon the young boy, including making him a Gentleman of the Bedchamber. In 1584, he was even asked to carry the crown at the opening of the Scottish parliament. Ludovick was a rising star, and by 1589, at the age of fifteen, he was made a member of the Scottish Privy Council. When the King went to Denmark to meet his bride, Ludovick was elected president of the Privy Council and was responsible for overseeing the subsequent wedding celebrations. Within a few years he had also been created the Lord High Admiral of Scotland. It is little wonder that, when James went to London as James I of England, Ludovick should go with him. He was appointed a member of the English Privy Council, First Gentleman of the Bedchamber and Lord Steward of the household. He had reached a very influential position, and all by the age of twenty-nine. Ludovick was rewarded well with Letters Patent; written orders directly issued by James:

from James I to Ludovick Stewart 2nd Duke of Lenox granting him the following lands at an annual rental of £66 8s 0¼d:-

The manor of Temple Newsam with free and copyhold rents; messuages and their appurtenances in Skelton, Colton Hall, Little Park, Colcoates, Osmondthorpe, Ellerker and Tunstall pastures in Temple Newsam, le Crooks Pightill Juxta Tunstall, Cole mines in Halton and Skelton: le Hospitall, the increased rents and profits of courts of the manor.

Also the manor of Settrinton co. York, and the manor of Wennesladale co. York, with agistment in the forest of Wennesladale, a further £10 pa being payable for the agistment.

(WYL100/NE/4, 31 May 1609)

Once more, the house was back in the custodianship of a private individual, albeit one with royal connections. The 2nd Duke of Lennox, as he then was, was quite an influential person in the court of King James. After he became a naturalised English subject in 1603, he went on to hold many positions of rank including, at various times, those of Ambassador to Scotland, King's Alnager, Lord High Commissioner for Scotland, Deputy Earl Marshall and Lord Steward of the Household. When the Prince of Wales, Henry, son of James, died unexpectedly in 1612, the heir presumptive became James's younger son, Charles. He was a sickly child and nobody expected him to achieve adulthood. James himself was ill and there was the very real prospect that, should he die, Charles would still be a minor and bring about a regency government. If this were to happen, then Ludovick was the nearest male relative of the King. Although a member of the English Privy Council, he was not a member of the English peerage and was therefore unable to sit in the Westminster parliament. This meant that he would not be able to take an active part in any regency administration. His proposal was that he should be raised to the peerage, and although this met with some initial opposition, he was created the 1st Earl of Richmond in 1613. However, this succession crisis passed without the necessity for a regent and Charles grew in strength to become king after the death of his father in 1625.

When James acceded to the throne, Ireland was still a mainly Gaelic speaking Catholic country. Under Henry VIII there had been a policy of Anglicising the Irish nobility, something that continued through the reigns of subsequent monarchs through to James. A nine-year-long insurrection was finally crushed in 1603, and many of the Irish nobility fled to the Continent. Their lands were now forfeit and James was presented with a plan for the 'Plantation of Ulster', which would see thousands of Protestant English and Scots resettled in Ireland. Land was granted to several English and Scots nobles, who became 'Undertakers' as they had to undertake certain conditions of settlement. Some of these were that they should build a fortified house and barn within three years and settle their land with a minimum of twenty-four Protestant men per 1,000 acres granted. These men would remain loyal to the King and be able to form a militia in times of trouble. The settlers were to represent at least ten families and each family had to build a stone house within the bounds of the fortified barn for defence purposes. In 1607, the Privy Council approved the resettlement of seized lands and Lennox was granted 2,000 acres of land in Donegal, where he 'planted' settlers from his Scottish estates. For him as Undertaker there were financial benefits. After five years, an Undertaker was liable to pay a tax of £5 6s 8d for every 1,000 acres held. Produce from the land could be exported for seven years free of tax and necessary goods imported free of tax for five years. It was also permissible for wood to be cut from the King's forests for building purposes.

As well as being involved in the Plantation of Ulster, Lennox was also a member of the Plymouth Council, established by James in 1620 to oversee the planting, ruling and governing of New England, in America, by the Plymouth Company (R.N. Worth, 1882). This was the period of the Pilgrim Fathers and James Smith of Pocahontas fame, stories that I grew up with as a young boy. It is amazing to think that the owner of Temple Newsam had direct links to these events, although it is very doubtful whether Lennox actually visited the Americas.

One might think that, with all these royal grants, subsidies and overseas business interests, Lennox was a wealthy man. He was however in constant financial difficulties. In 1614, he had mortgaged the estate for the sum of £9,000 (equivalent somewhere in the region of £860,000 today). The estate included not only the house and land but some smaller properties and at least two coal mines, as well as the profits of the manorial courts. Even this could not support Lennox, and in 1622, having no legitimate heirs, he began the sale of the estate to Sir Arthur Ingram for £12,000:

From the Earl and Countess of March [Duke of Lennox] acknowledging the receipt from Sir Arthur Ingram of £6,000 and good security for another £6,000 to be paid 'at several days to come' for the purchase of Temple Newsam manor and appurtenances.
(WYL100/NE/12a, 20 July 1622)

Unfortunately, it took Ingram a little longer than the 'several days to come' to conclude the payment. The sale was finally completed in July 1624, a few months after the death of the Duke.

From Esme Duke of Lenox Earl of March &c to Sir Arthur Ingram acknowledging receipt of £2,000, making £4,000 in all according to an indenture of 12 June, 1622. Also for several sums paid at divers times amounting to £10,000 over and above the present £2,000 making in all £12,000 being full price for the purchase of manor of Temple Newsam.

(WYL100/NE/12c, 4 July 1624)

For the first time in its history, the Temple Newsam estate had changed hands as a commercial enterprise. It had not been seized by the Crown or granted to the nobility; it was purely a business deal. And it is with Ingram that we witness the development of Temple Newsam House as we see it today, including the rebuilding of the north and south wings and the demolition of the east wing after a disastrous fire in 1635. It is only in the west wing that any of the original Tudor building remains. Ingram also had constructed in stone lettering the following saying around the roof line of the house:

ALL GLORY AND PRAISE BE GIVEN TO GOD THE FATHER THE SON AND THE HOLY GHOST, ON HIGH, PEACE UPON EARTH, GOOD WILL TOWARDS MEN, HONOUR AND TRUE ALLEGIANCE TO OUR GRACIOUS KING, LOVING AFFECTIONS AMONGST HIS SUBJECTS, HEALTH AND PLENTY WITHIN THIS HOUSE

Ingram was, if nothing else, ingratiating towards the King, as we shall see. The lettering is still there to be read today, a lasting testament to Ingram, although now the letters are of metal.

It is worth reflecting on Ingram's life as he is such an interesting character, and his story is very much a 'rags to riches' one. Born a Yorkshireman in about 1560, he was taken at an early age to London, where his father Hugh was a tallow chandler. This was a person who dealt in food commodities such as butter, cheese, flour, oatmeal and suchlike. Hugh Ingram made his money by importing his goods from the Continent and then retailing them. He was also involved in money lending and debt collecting. This was a common business occupation at the time and far removed from the seedy image we may have of a loan shark today. Arthur first appears in records in 1592 involved in the collection of debts.

Trade must have been good because he made enough money to put his eldest son, William, through Cambridge University. Arthur was destined to take over his father's business, which he did in about 1600. But he had his sights on higher things. He had a great deal of trading experience, a small amount of capital and, perhaps more significantly, some very useful business contacts. He became a civil servant; more specifically, he became a 'Waiter', the lowest rank of customs official. He must have been good at his work because within three years he had become a 'Controller', a principle customs officer in the port. There were four in the port of London, which handled the bulk of the country's shipping trade, so he was now in a respected position. The fact that he had been recommended to the Secretary of State, Robert Cecil, for his diligence might also have been influential in his rapid promotion.

His connection with Cecil opened many doors for him. Within a short space of time, Cecil was involving Ingram in many important financial affairs, such as overseeing the collection of duties on silk, velvets and Venetian silver and gold threads. This was a period when the Crown was becoming increasingly impoverished and any man who could raise money successfully was to be favoured. On the accession of James I, Cecil was using Ingram's help to push through a new fiscal policy. Still retaining his position as Controller, he was now acting as an advisor to the Secretary of State. He had access to relatively large sums of money, the patronage of the King's minister, and the possibility of giving valuable service to powerful and influential people. Ingram was a fixer and a contact man. He could bring together courtiers who had grants and money with businessmen who were willing to exploit them.

He was rewarded well for his services and began to amass wealth. He speculated to accumulate and invested in ventures such as the Virginia Company in the Americas and Raleigh's ill-fated expedition to Guiana; Raleigh sold Ingram a £330 share in his voyage (WYLEA/1/1 papers, 1592–1629). Much of his wealth was tied up in syndicates and capital investments and he was not frightened to borrow money when needed to further invest in the hope of making a profit. He was a ruthless businessman and seemed to care little for others. The Earl of Strafford, his one-time friend and patron, later wrote of him:

> I know well his avarice is sordid howbeit his wealth prodigious: of an insolent vainglorious nature, no honesty or rule to be had further than stands with his own gain, which is far nearer to him than any obligation or conscience: a man of no virtue or ability.
>
> (A.F. Upton, 1961)

Admittedly this was written after an argument between the two and may be slightly coloured on Strafford's part, but it is clear that Ingram was not universally well liked. Whether because of his nature or simply because people were jealous of his position, he attracted enemies. To be fair to his memory, he does appear to have had some softness to his character, as shown here in a letter to his third wife, Mary, in December 1621, complete with its Jacobean spelling and grammar:

> Swett hart, I have sent dyvers things to Hull the which I would gladly have att home before Cryssmas. [Many items were sent by sea to Hull rather than risk the long and sometimes dangerous land journey.] I pray you send one of purpose to Jno Mattison [Mattison was Ingram's Steward] and let him gow over to Hull. The Mr of the ship is nam is Thomas Collinson. Yff the watter should be so ffrosen that he can nott com up the Ryver to York, then would I gladly have them brought in a wayn, especially the cask wher in the wyn and the gamms of bacon and anchoves and picell oysters and ullyves [olives] and cappers [capers] that the bee lickwiss brought up, of thes things good Swett hart be a littell carefull, and so I rest in haste being gowing to the court your very loving husband.
>
> (P. Robinson, 1926)

He had a finger in many pies. Ingram was involved with arms dealing, in exporting British artillery to the Continent; he was sent to Ireland to investigate corrupt and inefficient customs practices; he was part of a syndicate that held a monopoly on the importation of tropical dye-wood; he was influential in appropriating the Yorkshire alum industry for the Crown; and for a short time, another of his syndicates held the monopoly on the importation of tobacco, before they sold their rights for £4,000.

Some of Ingram's activities were somewhat dubious. He was not afraid of a bit of wheeler-dealing if there was a profit to be made. On one occasion, a number of barrels of indigo and cochineal, originally pirated goods, found their way into the hands of Ingram and his syndicate. He played a crafty game and declared them as being pirated but the syndicate was allowed to keep them provided it paid the appropriate customs duties. This they did, and then sold on the products for a handsome profit.

King James was an impoverished king. He was desperate for money and Ingram, amongst others, was influential in raising much needed capital as well as lining his own pockets. He was rewarded for his service to the King by being knighted in 1613. But his personal aspirations almost led to his downfall. In an ambitious attempt to gain office and power, he made a bid to buy the position of Cofferer of the Royal Household. This was an important and influential post because it allowed the holder to handle the money involved in running the court and also the possibility of great moneymaking schemes. The Cofferer also had influence and could confer favours on those connected with the court. This was an important aspect for his backers and promoters. Under a cloak of secrecy he bought out the incumbent, Sir Robert Vernon, for an agreed sum and an annuity for life. Figures vary, but it is certain that Ingram paid between £1,500 and £2,500, with an annuity of between £500 and £600. Once this had been settled in the February, preparations for his installation were begun, again in close secrecy. The other officers of the household were dismayed at his appointment when they became aware of it. Ingram was not of genteel birth; he was a tradesman; an upstart. The King had promised that all positions within the household would descend according to the rules of seniority. Many officers, themselves having invested significant money in acquiring their positions, felt cheated and made personal protests to the King. Feelings ran high:

> in an age that was acutely conscious of caste and status, they bitterly resented the pretensions of such a parvenu to hold office with them, and share with them common social life, and be treated as their equal,

when he had no shadow of a claim to gentle birth, and had acquired a sinister personal reputation.

(A.F. Upton, 1926)

Such was the bitterness after his appointment that his fellow officers went on strike and refused to have anything to do with him! The war of words continued while Ingram took up residence at court. Some of his promoters realised their own sensitive positions and withdrew, leaving mainly the Howard family in support. Ingram was offered a way out. He would retain his title and position until such time as his payment for the office was refunded. He would not handle funds or take his place at table when the court dined. Ingram would not back down and continued stubbornly in office until the July, when bowing to pressure he reluctantly agreed to the terms and conceded defeat. He must have felt shame and humiliation. He had learned that it was not for a common born man to break into the realms of the gentry, no matter how much wealth he might have. It was perhaps the greatest misfortune he had faced but with true resilience of character he shrugged it off and looked to his future – in the north.

Although he had spent most of his life in London, Ingram had an affinity with the north of England. He was, after all, a Yorkshireman by birth and he had bought some Crown lands in the north as investments. He had also spent time in Yorkshire when dealing with the alum industry and around this time, in 1612, he had bought the position of Secretary to the Council of the North. The council was an administrative body acting as a provincial government in support of London. The post of secretary was salaried, with further benefits from a range of fees charged for a variety of services; Ingram always had an eye on the profits. Putting the events of 1615 behind him, he moved north to establish his position in society there.

He already had a lease on a house in York but now he invested some of his wealth into building a new large residence in the area of the former Bishop's palace in the city. At the same time as this was being built, Ingram was also investing in the building of a country house at Sherriff Hutton, some 10 miles east of York, on a site near the ruined castle. Ingram had already bought most of the Forest of Galtre, in which Sherriff Hutton is situated. King James himself was entertained at a hunting party at Sherriff Hutton.

Ingram's status within the county was growing rapidly. He had office on the Council of the North, he had strong connections to the London court and he was well acquainted with many noble families. He was wealthy and was able to issue contracts and hand out jobs, and the Yorkshire woollen industry relied upon him for the supply of alum. He was a man of some importance. So much so that by 1619, he was made High Sherriff of Yorkshire, and a few years later, in 1624, he was Member of Parliament for York, a position he held until 1629, when Charles I dissolved Parliament for eleven years.

Throughout his career he had benefitted from a close association with the Court and, although he was always looking for ways to profit and make advancement, he did support the monarchy. However, his Protestant zeal and religious convictions were evident. He had a hatred of popery and upheld the virtues and importance of preaching. In fact, as a Member of Parliament he was considered to be an expert on the subject and was often consulted. His charitable works included arranging a weekly sermon to be preached to the inmates of York prison, although to what effect is not recorded. Ingram appears to have had some sympathy for the plight of prisoners and was involved in the investigation into accusations of abuse by the warden of the Fleet Prison in London. Why he had such an interest in the Fleet is not known. He had no direct connection with it, although it is speculated that perhaps some of his former debtors had ended up there and he felt some form of guilt. It was while this investigation was underway that he became embroiled in the case of Edward Floyd, a recusant barrister languishing in the Fleet. After the 'Protestant disaster' of 1621 in Bohemia, an area of the Czech Republic in which many Protestant estate leaders were publicly executed and their lands given to loyal Catholics, Floyd was heard speaking in support of this. Ingram was instructed to search his belongings and reported to Parliament that a variety of popish artefacts had been found – a rosary, relics and a crucifix, amongst others. He was arraigned before the House of Commons, where various brutal punishments were demanded, such as branding or having his nose and ears cut off. Ingram took no active part in this attack, which in some ways was fortunate for him because it was realised that Floyd was not a member of the House and could therefore not be punished by them. He avoided embarrassment once more by judiciously not involving himself in the post-Bohemia hysteria.

On the accession of Charles I, Ingram's relationship with Crown and Parliament wavered between loyalty to the monarch and support for the revolutionary ideals. Certainly during the Scottish troubles of 1637, and after, he was loyal to the Crown and was actively engaged in raising funds for the campaign. By 1641, the crisis was deepening and England was slipping steadily towards civil war. Ingram now had more sympathy with Parliament. His name appeared on a list of the 'Protestation against popery' and he was one of the members who presented the revolutionary proposals to the House of Lords, defining the intention to take executive control for the King. Later in 1641 he was one of the twelve who attended the King at Hampton Court to present the 'Grand Remonstrance', which was a summary of Parliament's opposition to the King's policies on religious, financial, legal and foreign matters. The King did not accept the objections and, as reconciliation appeared impossible, England slid steadily towards civil war.

By early 1642, Ingram was a militant supporter of Parliament. He sat on committees to prepare the kingdom for defence; to organise gunpowder or troops guarding the Houses of Lords and Commons; and to investigate a plot to seize the magazine at Hull. But Ingram was ill. The last time he appeared in the House of Commons was 20 May, and he returned to Yorkshire in the June. Two days after the King had raised his royal standard in Nottingham on 22 August, Ingram died, and was buried in York Minster. His will endowed a hospital in Bootham, York, and he left instructions that a set of candlesticks be presented to the Minster after his death.

However, financial matters dogged the Ingram family, even after Sir Arthur's death. In October 1645, Sir Arthur Ingram junior received a letter from Whitehall demanding to know what he was going to do concerning the £3,550 plus accrued interest that was due on his father's estate in November 1642. The letter goes on to warn him that:

I am advised by Counsell ... that your father's bond of £8,000 be put in suit against you.

(WYL100/C4 WYAS, 3 October 1645)

A serious matter indeed, but it is unclear what the results were of these demands. Did Sir Arthur Ingram junior pay off his father's debts or did financial problems continue? We do know not. What is known is that money problems appear to have continued down the Ingram line. A tantalising hint is given in a letter from 'H.' Ingram to a Mr Ellison in 1647:

Mr Lindley will acquaint you if Mr Matteson have not with some moneys to be delivered to Will. Pell for you, to my use. I desire you to call of Will. Pell for it, for you will find it sealed as with my seal in two bags, if upon view you think it to be right, I pray you to deliver it unopened, if otherwise let it be counted over before you deliver Will. Pell this note, if he make payment and recording to his Bill, you are to give him 1s for the carriage of it; he hath a Trunke likewise corded and directed to you marked with nails; 1642 [coincidentally, the year Sir Arthur Ingram died]. ... The case is now alterd my brother Ar. Tells me ye committee at Goldsmith Hall hath sent an inquest after him and me and divers others, as delinquents. Therefore I desire you and Mr Lindley to confir that had best be done with my goods. I think it is not safe to send them to Mr Cockings, before my wife come, lest it be knowne, and they maybe sequestered, but wither lest they be kept, in your or my house as his, or in some other privat place until you heare farther from mee, this news hath a little blundered me.

[signed] H. Ingram
(WYL100/C4 WYAS, 17 April 1647)

Earlier in 1647, 'H.' had written to Sir Arthur Ingram junior stating that:

You partly know in what desperate condition my debt is. ... After your father's death ... to consider what you will give me, whether all, anything, or nothinge at all, yet I will rest satisfied with your love ... let us make the reckoning straight. ... I pray you, let me have your answer or if you desire, to speake with me, let me know when & I will waite on you. God bless you & yours

[signed] Your friend & faithfull kinsman H.
(WYL100/C4 WYAS, 6 January 1647)

The names are a little confusing, and in the first letter, 'H.' refers to his brother Ar. (Arthur). 'H.' could be Henry, the first Viscount Irwin and brother to Arthur Ingram III (son of Sir Arthur Ingram junior). In the second letter to an Arthur Ingram, 'H.' refers to the death of *your* father; not our father. The implication of this is that this Arthur Ingram is his uncle, Sir Arthur Ingram junior. 'H.' clearly had run up debts somehow and felt that he was due something from the estate of his grandfather. An astute businessman, Sir Arthur Ingram would have been dismayed.

Ingram was not to see the horror of a war in which Englishman fought Englishman. Neither was he to witness the defeat of the King and his subsequent execution. But, had he lived, there is little doubt that he would have been involved. However, although he may not have lived through the events of the civil war, his sons did and the Ingram house was a house divided.

Arthur Ingram junior, the elder son, like his father, was a loyal Parliamentarian. He inherited the estate at Temple Newsam and continued the building and renovation work on the house. He was a High Sherriff of Yorkshire and a Justice of the Peace for the county. He also sat in the House of Commons and was knighted in 1621. His brother Thomas, on the other hand, was an ardent Royalist. He lived on the Ingram's estate at Sherriff Hutton. Knighted in 1636, he was Member of Parliament for Thirsk, in North Yorkshire, and sat in the Long Parliament in 1640. He was disabled from sitting in the House in 1642, and in the same year, was given the Commission for Array by the King. This meant that he had been given the task of mustering the inhabitants of the county to expand the Royalist army in preparation for the conflict that was now inevitable. When hostilities began he sought shelter in Newark garrison and claimed that he had lost £5,000 to plundering. A supporter of the royal court in exile, he sent £1,000 to France and was instrumental in negotiations to bring the young King Charles II back to England. After the Restoration of the monarchy in 1660, he was re-elected to Parliament for Thirsk and sat in the so-called Cavalier Parliament. Sir Thomas was highly favoured by the King and was created Chancellor of the Duchy of Lancaster in 1664 and a member of the Privy Council, a position he kept until his death in 1672. His tomb in Westminster Abbey bears witness to his service to the monarchy:

Here lies interr'd (in full assurance of a glorious Resurrection) the body of ye Right Honble. Thomas Ingram Knt. Who for his eminent loyalty, suffering and services to & for theire Majesties King Charles ye 1st & the 2nd was (by ye latter) made Chancellor of the Duchy of Lancaster, and one of His Most Honble. Privy Council

The Ingrams were without a doubt an influential family in the fabric of seventeenth-century British history. Although the acquisition of Temple Newsam was just one of the many properties Sir Arthur Ingram senior gathered to his overall holdings in the north of England, it is a measure of the estate's importance that it became the seat of the Ingrams for many years.

Sir Arthur Ingram senior was, in today's terminology, a self-made man. He came from humble origins but through drive and ambition, and perhaps with a little guile and sharp practice, he rose to high office. Yes, he was ruthless; but what successful businessman isn't? He was possibly not the most likeable of men, but success often breeds arrogance. Yet it is a measure of his grit and determination that, coming from lowly beginnings, he achieved so much.

He and his sons left us the truly wonderful legacy of Temple Newsam House and estate. Walking around the house, strolling from room to room, opens the door into his world; a world we can still experience today.

Chapter 5

A Landscaped House

The debt to Lancelot 'Capability' Brown

The current house that we visit today is really a palimpsest of ideas
and styles, each one being added to the previous. What at first sight
appears old is often not so. For example, the famous Oak Staircase,
although appearing Tudor in style is a much later nineteenth-century
addition. Of the original Tudor house built by Lord Darcy, very little
remains. There are some clues left in the largely undisturbed cellars, where
Tudor doorways can still be seen along with possible remains of the original
timberwork. Some Tudor carving can also be found in the Bretton Room.
The west wing of the house still follows the lines of the original building but
the rest was considerably modelled and remodelled by successive owners.

When Sir Arthur Ingram senior took ownership of the house he immediately
began the redesigning work. The south and north wings were rebuilt, and
the east wing was demolished after a disastrous fire in 1635. The Tudor west
wing was absorbed into Ingram's new designs. It was a significantly large
household. A 1667 inventory records that 'Temple Newsam House had sixty-
six rooms and eleven outhouses' (WYL100/EA/3/11). A coloured engraving
by the Dutch draughtsmen Johannes Kip and Leonard Knyff, published
in *Britannia Illustrata* (1707), gives a bird's-eye view of the house and its
immediate surroundings as it would have appeared some years after Ingram's
death. The engraving was published when Ingram's grandson, Henry Ingram,
was created Viscount Irwine (sometimes written as Irwin, Irvine or Irving) by
Charles II. It is orientated with the east–west axis running from bottom to top
and the south–north axis running from left to right. An original version of this
plate was produced in 1699, but we can say that by the end of the seventeenth
century there had been some major alterations to the original Tudor body of
the house. It is clear that the original Tudor courtyard house is now in the

fashionable 'half-H' style (R. Roberts, 2010). The east wing, destroyed by fire, has been replaced by a low wall with a central arched gateway flanked by two gatehouses. The Steward's Accounts for the 1630s gives an entry for '1s 8d paid for a centre for ye gates' (WYL100/EA/13/39).

Could this have been when the arch, as shown in the engraving, was created for the gateway? Certainly it is known that Ingram purchased lead to cover the gatehouses and laid new boards for support at around this time. The archway itself is reminiscent of the style of seventeenth-century architect Inigo Jones. Jones had carried out work for Ingram's long-term friend, partner and rival Lionel Cranfield, the Earl of Middlesex. The three of them were well known to each other so it is not inconceivable that perhaps Jones supplied the plans for the archway, even if he was not directly instrumental in its construction for Ingram. Kip's engraving of Temple Newsam shows architectural features very much favoured by Jones, with symmetrical outlines and pilastered facades all in keeping with the new Palladian style. In 2007, Heritage Technology Ltd created a 3D reconstruction of the exterior of Temple Newsam House for a 'Work and Play' exhibition. Basing their designs on the 1699 Kip engraving, the images clearly show how the house may have looked at that time.

One feature on the engraving has remained something of a puzzle. To the south-west of the south wing is a separate brick building. This has been referred to as the Banqueting Hall and R. Strong (1979) considers this to be the one that Ingram constructed in the 1630s. Documents held in the West Yorkshire Archives record that in 1633, a bricklayer named John Wilton was employed to:

> add erect and build one peece of brick building on the southside of the Kitchin at Temple Newsam ... iiiis xd the rood and to be paid upon measure of every storye, the wall to be 2 foote and a halfe in bredth ... also to make a brick wall on the backside of the house of offices for an orchard at the said house of Temple Newsam 70 yds in length and 42 yds in breadth and 3 yds in height, at 3s -d a rood, wall to be 10 ft in height round. To be paid every fortnight for the wall and every storey for the brick building.
>
> (WYL100/EA/13/71/4, 7 August 1633)

Certainly the original kitchens were situated in the basement of the south wing, although later relocated to the north wing. Subsequent explorations have revealed foundations of a building on the site as indicated in the Kip engraving, so the engraving is probably quite an accurate representation of the house at that time.

When looking at Temple Newsam an interesting factor to consider is that it is built of brick. There was a distinct north-south divide when it came to building materials for large buildings such as Temple Newsam. Of what your home was constructed was clearly a reflection of your status. In earlier times, houses had been built largely of wood, but by the seventeenth century, wooden structures were equated with a lower status. Stone and brick were now the desired choices. In the south of England there was often a lack of quality stone for building. What there was had to be quarried and then transported, often adding to the costs of construction. Consequently, many large houses built in the south were of brick. Bricks were a commodity that could be created on site or locally, cutting labour and transport costs significantly. A contract between Ingram and certain brick makers refers to bricks being delivered 'into the kilns where they usually burn them in the said ground' (WYL100/EA/17/31/5, 20 October 1636), indicating that bricks were being fired on site. However, in the north of the country, stone was readily available, especially in Yorkshire, where Ingram had several of his properties. He did use stone for garden ornaments, balustrading and chimneys; this was obtained from Huddlestone quarry near Tadcaster, equidistant from his properties in York and Temple Newsam. On occasions he sent his carver, Thomas Ventris, to select and cut stone for use at Temple Newsam. But his favoured material was brick: red Hatfield-style brick. Was this a conscious desire to imitate the affluent south or was it simply cost effective to use locally produced brick against the costs of acquiring the stone? Certainly brick was seen as an advantageous and desirable material, even as early as the fifteenth century:

I confess, I believe that at first men were put upon making Bricks to supply the Place of Stone in their Buildings, thro' Scarcity and Want of it; but afterwards finding how ready they were in Working, how well adapted both to Use and Beauty, how strong and durable, they proceeded to make not only their ordinary Structures, but even their Palaces of Brick. ... I will be bold to say, that there is not a better Material for any Sort of Edifice than Brick.

(Alberti, 1955)

Buildings made from stone were from the medieval mindset. They were fortresses and castles and lacked some of the architectural finesse of the seventeenth century. Stone was suitable for buildings that embodied power and strength but brick allowed for more subtlety and grace. The brick-built palaces and mansions displayed wealth, status and an aesthetic taste, something that Ingram aspired to. Although Yorkshire stone was readily available, it is interesting to consider that his properties in Yorkshire were built of brick.

Brick making was a skilled craft, first seen in Hull in the fourteenth century. It was a commercial industry and in 1630, Ingram's steward, John Matteson, wrote to his master that he had bought 4,000 bricks for the building work in York at the price of eleven shillings and sixpence per 1,000 (WYL178/5). Only one year later, Matteson purchased 150,000 bricks for the Temple Newsam construction at the price of three shillings and four pence per 1,000 – a considerable difference (A. Upton, 1961). Even at the lower rate, Ingram was paying £25 (approximately £2,500 today) for bricks for Temple Newsam as opposed to the outlay of £2.30 (approximately £220 today) for his property in York. An interesting comparison is that 1,000 bricks today can cost anywhere from £240 to £338, depending on quality and style.

Whatever reasons Ingram chose to use red brick, whether financial, social, or even a combination of both, he began the process of transforming the original Tudor building into the building that we would recognise today. This process continued for the next century, spanning all incumbent Viscounts Irwin, from Henry Ingram, grandson of Arthur Ingram senior and created the first Viscount in 1661, to Charles Ingram, who succeeded as the ninth and last Viscount Irwin in 1763 on the death of his uncle.

Charles Ingram was an eligible bachelor who caught the eye of the young Frances Shepheard (sometimes written as Shepherd). She was the natural daughter of the wealthy Tory, Samuel Shepheard. Although he never married her mother (she was actually born Frances Gibson), he left Frances a wealthy inheritance of £40,000 in his will on the proviso that she would not marry an Irishman, a Scot, a peer or the son of a peer (www.historyofparliamentonline.org). What he had against the Irish, Scots or peers of the realm is not known. Under the terms of the will, Frances had been made a ward of court and it was after some years of legal wrangling between lawyers that a marriage settlement was finally agreed on 2 August 1758 (WYL100/F/17/50), although records show that she and Charles actually married on 28 June 1758 (www.ancestry.co.uk). Frances fell in love with Temple Newsam House and it was at her insistence that the famed Lancelot 'Capability' Brown became involved with the estate. 'Capability' Brown was nicknamed so because he was reputed to always see the 'capability' of a landscape.

During the early part of the eighteenth century, fashions within garden design were changing. The more formal garden layout, as designed for Sir Arthur Ingram by the architect and designer William Etty, was giving way to a new train of thought. There was a desire for a more natural composition, giving the illusion of what was now being seen in Italian classic landscape paintings. Informality, asymmetry and naturalism were the vogue and the creation of a 'natural' setting was to become an art under Lancelot Brown. His style was also known as 'picturesque' because it sought to emulate the classic landscape pictures. The style was rolling grassland, clumps and scatterings of trees, and manmade serpentine lakes.

The philosopher Jean-Jacques Rousseau was perhaps the most influential of all 'Enlightenment' writers of the period and his thoughts on the relationship between man and nature were to have far-reaching effects, especially in attitudes towards landscaping. In 1761, he wrote a book entitled *Julie, or the New Heloise*. Although a work of fiction, it embodied his philosophies and greatly influenced the Romantic-Naturalism movement of the eighteenth century. He developed the idea of a return to the rustic simplicity of rural life and promulgated the cult of the shepherdess. For the elite of eighteenth-century society the figures of the shepherd and shepherdess achieved cult status. Masqued balls were frequently attended by those dressed accordingly, and these Arcadian figures became heroes of fashionable plays and poetry. Frances Shepheard Ingram was painted as a shepherdess by Benjamin Wilson, and this portrait can be seen today in

Temple Newsam House. Here she is shown, crook in hand, in a pastoral setting. Perhaps it was also intended as a pun on her maiden name of Shepheard.

The artistic creation of nature underpins much of the philosophy of the age. In *Julie*, Rousseau writes:

> Nature has done it all, but under my direction, and there is nothing here that I have not ordered.

This could have perhaps become Brown's mantra, for his work was to create the illusion of natural growth, and it is a testament to the success of much of his work that it is not always possible to identify the created from the natural. One can quite forgive visitors today looking out from Temple Newsam House across the parkland and viewing a seemingly natural environment, but much of it was created and landscaped during the eighteenth century.

Lancelot Brown was born in Northumberland in 1716. Having completed his apprenticeship as a gardener he set out for the south of England, with great ambitions. By 1741, he had become the head gardener at Stowe Park, in Buckinghamshire. In 1750, he embarked on what is often referred to as his 'great ride'. He travelled across the west of England, taking in the large estates and discussing with their owners the potential for developing their parklands. He took on many important commissions and, with a growing portfolio of work, he was now able to consider an independent career as a landscape artist. Brown had a fascination with water and water features; not the ornamental type but natural appearing features such as lakes and rivers. He would often plan for a series of serpentine linked lakes with dams and mock bridges that gave the appearance of a meandering river through the undulating grassland. All of this was carefully constructed, using the topography of the land wherever possible, but many of the lakes had to be dug out by hard labour. Wet clay formed the lining of these lakes and the clay had to be 'puddled', compressing it until all the air was squeezed out to form a solid watertight layer. He often used a flock of sheep driven backwards and forwards across the clay until their small hooves had compressed the surface enough.

Brown's client list grew to include dukes and duchesses, several prime ministers and many members of the House of Lords. It is little wonder then that Frances Shepheard Ingram wanted Lancelot Brown to work at Temple Newsam. Frances was a lover of the Italian classic landscape artists and there were several in her collection. She wanted the grounds of Temple Newsam to be like one of these pastoral settings and Brown's distinctive style met her desires. The key features of his work included:

- The house to be emphasised by standing alone with lawns sweeping up to the walls
- Gravel paths winding through shrubberies
- A ha-ha, or sunken ditch, to allow uninterrupted views across the parkland
- Clumps of trees drawing the eye towards a lake or 'river'
- Occasional hidden temples or other architectural features
- A carriage drive that followed a circuitous route and that allowed impressive views of the house
- Serpentine lakes, sometimes linked, giving the illusion of a river.

Many of these features were created at Temple Newsam and can still be seen today.

However, engaging the services of this very popular man was somewhat problematic. Shortly after the Ingrams' wedding in 1758, they requested Brown to make a visit to Temple Newsam to discuss the proposals. He was currently working on a project at Harewood House, to the north of Leeds, and informed them politely that he would be unavailable until the following summer. People clamoured for his thoughts and ideas. Earlier in that year, William Teesdale wrote to Samuel Popplewell, the steward of Harewood House, asking 'for any thoughts that has drop'd from the Great Man' (WYL250/SCZ/2/59).

Clearly he was the man of the moment, although there were others working in the field of landscaping at this time, such as Adam Mickle and Richard Woods. Brown's foreman, Thomas White, would also become an independent landscape designer in the latter half of the century. He became enthused with the commercial growing of timber for pit props in the coal mines of Yorkshire and Nottinghamshire. One of Brown's advantages over other landscape artists of the period was that his fees were never extortionate. He had even been known to draw up plans at no cost if he deemed the client worthy of such a charitable act. The Earl of Coventry wrote of him: 'I think he has studied both my Place & Pocket' (CR125B/153).

Brown's method of working was to usually send one of his men or a local surveyor to make a site visit. It was not often that Brown made the initial visit himself. After the site visit and the surveyor's report he would then draw up detailed plans, and prepare a contract with estimates of costs, labour and materials. It was at this point that direct discussions with the client would be made. In 1760, Drummond's Bank accounts record a single payment by Viscount Irwin to Lancelot Brown for the sum of £40. Clearly Brown had carried out some initial work on the project. Possibly this was an initial payment for Brown to begin making the plans because it is known that he visited the Viscount and his wife in 1763 and Brown's detailed master plans are dated the same year. The plans for Temple Newsam are only one of two of his plans still in existence; the other being for Sledmere House near Driffield, in the East Riding of Yorkshire.

Temple Newsam was only one of many ongoing projects that Brown was undertaking at this time. Viscount Irwin was in good company. Brown's only surviving account book dates from this period and shows that he was carrying out work for His Majesty the King (George III), the Duke of Bridgewater, the Earl of Coventry, the Duke of Marlborough, the 2nd Earl Gower, the 3rd Earl of Shelburne and several knights of the realm. It is estimated that his income for 1764 amounted to at least £6,000 (approximately £450,000 today) and by 1768, his account at Drummonds held £32,000 (approximately £2.5 million today), although he did have to pay an increasing number of foremen. He was undoubtedly a busy and wealthy man!

Some initial work was begun in the plantation as early as 1760, but it was not until 1765 that it becomes clear that Brown was ready to implement his plans. In a letter to his wife in May of that year, the Viscount informed her that: 'Mr Brown is ready to perform whenever it is agreeable and will bring a man for that purpose immediately' (WYL100/C/19/146a).

But it was not until October 1765 that the work finally began, under the watchful eye of Brown's foreman, William Stone. Unfortunately, it was an inclement autumn and heavy rains hindered progress of the work. Frances herself commented in a letter:

We have had a long continuance of fine weather but at length the rain is come which I am very sorry for as my Lord has just begun with Mr Brown & wet weather is very unfavourable for their operations.

The implications of the wording of the letter are that Brown himself was present at Temple Newsam, and that Viscount Irwin was also actively involved. This is quite possible as it is known that the Viscount was interested in varieties of new plants and was particularly interested in the propagation of pineapples. A hothouse within the walled garden was created to the east of the Home Farm. Pineapples were becoming fashionable fruits during the eighteenth century and were often considered a symbol of wealth. They were at first put out for display on dinner tables rather than being eaten, and then re-used several times before they would begin to rot. During the latter half of the century there was often a great rivalry between aristocrats as to who could produce the best pineapples.

Frances was also active in the garden, supervising the planting, which she sometimes referred to as 'Brownification'. The progress of the work was recorded by Frances in several letters over the period. In April 1766, she referred to the weather as being summer-like and that: 'I am out of doors all day long. Mr Brown has put us in a woful [*sic*] dirty pickle but my gravel walk is always a resource and very much made use of.'

Later in July, she recorded that Brown had left Temple Newsam but that work was continuing as there was much still to be done. By February 1767, the poor weather meant that there was little she could actively do and she 'stood still while Col Pitt & my husband have been Brownifying my dear gravel walk, his little wife carried stakes for them to mark out places for shrubs & I stood by to give my approbation.'

Viscount Irwin may have been getting his hands dirty but it was certainly Frances who had the final say as to where things were to be planted!

Viscount Irwin's bank records show that Brown was paid until September 1771, with a final payment of £570 (in excess of £36,000 today). Was the work completed? Well, not entirely. Much of Brown's plans submitted in 1763 were carried out. The rigid geometrical design as shown in the Kip engraving had been transformed. The avenue to the east of the house was now gone and a plantation established in its place. The southern aspect still retained a more formal garden, with walkways, but the Banqueting Hall and the riding school were gone. The original eastern approach designed by William Etty had been partially kept. The straight approach across the stone bridges was retained but Brown now gave the carriageway a sinuous bend so that the distant house disappeared behind trees only to be seen again in all its glory as the carriageway emerged. The northern approach was also altered, with visitors entering through two sphinx-topped gates constructed in 1768. The Rotunda, so clearly seen on the original plans nestling in the wooded hillside above the lakes, finally appeared as a small colonnaded Greek temple.

It is the lake and its associated features that were the main points missing from Brown's original plan. The present sequence of three lakes is not Brown's creation. A painting by James Chapman from about 1750 shows the eastern aspect of Temple Newsam as it may have been intended after Brown's works had been completed. The stable block to the right still exists but the riding school on the left was demolished. Rolling grassland sweeps up towards the house but there is a large lake set before the house, and this never materialised. The lake seen in the foreground could be the present-day lake. Another painting by Michael 'Angelo' Rooker, of 1765, also gives a view of the eastern aspect of the house from the ornamental temple as if Brown's plans had been completed.

In 1767, the clergyman and author Sydney Swinney dedicated a poem to Lord Irwin. In this somewhat lengthy work he praises Temple Newsam and the work of Brown:

> *But you, my Lord, at Temple Newsam find,*
> *The charms of nature gracefully combin'd*
> *Sweet waving hills, with wood and verdure crown'd*
> *And winding vales, where murmuring streams resound:*
> *Slopes fring'd with Oaks which gradual die away,*
> *And all around romantic scenes display.*
> *Delighted still along the park we rove,*
> *Vary'd with Hill and Dale, with Wood and Grove:*
> *O'er velvet Lawns what noble Prospects rise,*
> *Fair as the Scenes that Ruben's hand supplies.*
> *But when the Lake that these sweet Grounds adorn,*

And bright expanding like the eye of Morn,
Reflects whate'er above its surface rise,
The hills, the Rocks, the Woods and varying Skies,
Then will the wild and beautiful combine,
And taste in Beauty grace your whole Design.
But you Great Artist, like the source of light,
Gilds every scene with beauty and delight;

The poem then goes on to detail some of Brown's other landscape works, before ending with these lines:

At his command a new creation blooms;
Born to grace Nature, and her works complete,
With all that's beautiful, sublime and great;
For him each Muse enwreathes the Laurel Crown,
And consecrates to Fame immortal Brown.

(S. Swinney, Temple Newsam collection)

Praise indeed to have one's work immortalised in this manner and, like some of the paintings we have already mentioned, it alludes to the realisation of a plan that was never fully completed.

The death of the Viscount in 1778 was probably the reason why Brown never completed his commission. Frances lived on at the house until 1807, and although she may have been the driving force behind the 'Brownification' of Temple Newsam, after the death of her husband, she appears to have lacked the enthusiasm she once had. We can only guess what Temple Newsam may have looked like had Brown completed his work, but he did leave us with an example of the quintessentially 'Jardin Anglaise', as it became known in France and elsewhere on the Continent.

Brown had created a style of English garden that reflected the mood of the time. Landscaped gardens were promoted as a national patriotic style of art. Prime Minister William Pitt the Elder once instructed Brown to 'Go you and adorn England.' He did, and in his career he created around 250 different landscapes, of which 150 are still viewable today.

Temple Newsam was just one of fourteen projects he undertook in Yorkshire. It may not have been completed but, as you wander around the grounds of the great house, it is not too difficult to imagine Lancelot Brown doffing his hat to you as he strides across the parkland in his green worsted coat. The inspiration and enthusiasm of the Viscount Irwin and his wife Frances, and the capability of Lancelot Brown, shaped the landscape of Temple Newsam that we see today.

Chapter 6

A Scandalous House

The Marchioness of Hertford and the Prince Regent

Temple Newsam has had a long history of connection with royalty, either being owned directly by the Crown itself or through its ownership by members of the extended royal family of the period. It is not certain if earlier monarchs ever visited the estate, but it is known for certain that George, Prince of Wales, later to become the Prince Regent and King George IV, visited in 1806. The circumstances of his visit are intriguing and we shall come to those shortly.

At the turn of the eighteenth century, Britain was in turmoil. King George II had been on the throne since 1760, and during this time England had been through the Seven Years' War, had lost its American colony to independence, was engaged with France in further conflict, and was facing revolution in Ireland. On the domestic front, political struggles dogged his life. The rivalry between the two political parties, the Whigs and Tories, would be a source of constant friction. As a monarch, he would naturally be inclined to support the Tory Party, which stood for the maintenance of the status quo, with the King as supreme authority. The Whigs, in comparison, stood for reform and a more liberal attitude, with power resting with the people. Indeed, when the French Revolution broke out in 1789, Charles Fox, a leading reformer politician of the Whig Party, hailed the event as being the greatest that had happened in world history. In addition to this, the King had shown, in 1788, early signs of an illness that would plague him for the rest of his reign. Bouts of irrational and violent behaviour were common and in one incident on 5 November of that year, he attacked his eldest son, George, smashing his head against a wall. Fortunately, this first round of illness lasted only a short time and although George, the Prince of Wales, attempted to wrest power from his ill father, the King's recovery put a stop to this.

The behaviour of George, his eldest son, was also a constant worry to the King. Some say that this was a contributory factor to the King's illness, although this has never been proven. George had a complex and dissolute character. By the age of seventeen he had begun an affair with Mary Robinson, an actress and a married woman, although it is rumoured that he may have had an earlier liaison with his sister's governess, Mary Hamilton. Wearing his 'heart on his sleeve', the Prince convinced himself that he was madly in love with Mrs Robinson and sent her endless letters and gifts. The affair lasted only a year and was not altogether well received by the public, who were made aware of the liaison through the press. Mrs Robinson had kept many of the Prince's letters to her and threatened to expose him when he began to reject her in favour of a Mrs Armistead. Mrs Robinson had run up enormous debts during her time with the Prince and eventually, much to the relief of court circles, she agreed to hand over the letters for the sum of £5,000. The Prince meanwhile continued his philandering ways. Brief affairs with a Mrs Dalrymple, rumoured to have conceived his child, and the Countess von Hardenberg, only brought more trouble for the King.

The taking of mistresses by royalty and the nobility was not exactly uncommon; indeed, it was almost accepted by most, as long as it was discreet. However, the Prince of Wales was not exactly the soul of discretion. Alternating between fits of manic euphoria and bouts of deep depression, he fell in and out of love regularly. He would become so enamoured of a woman that if she did not respond to his advances he would become so depressed that he would threaten or even attempt suicide. His affair with the widowed Mrs Fitzherbert caused the greatest upset. He begged to marry her and when she at first rejected him he drank himself into a stupor. Hearing that she was about to leave for the Continent, he stabbed himself with a sword and summoned her to him. Seeing his bleeding body, and coupled with his repeated requests to marry him, she relented and reluctantly agreed. Here was the problem: Mrs Fitzherbert was a Catholic, and the 1701 Act of Settlement dictated that only a Protestant unencumbered with a Catholic wife could inherit the throne. This was reinforced by the 1772 Royal Marriage Act, which forbade any descendants of the late George II from marrying without the specific consent of His Majesty and his heirs. Mrs Fitzherbert did leave for Europe and the Prince wanted to follow her, but the

King would not grant him permission to travel abroad due to his reckless conduct and the amount of debt he had built up. Eventually she returned and they were married in a clandestine ceremony on 15 December 1785, and it was carried out under the rites of the Church of England. It was not long before rumours of the marriage began to spread in the press and the matter of the Prince's general conduct was placed for debate in Parliament. Whilst privately supporting the Prince, many politicians recognised the potential dangers caused by the marriage. This was at a time when there were still many prejudices against Catholics, and the Catholic Emancipation Act had yet to be passed. It had serious implications for the succession of the monarchy and there was a fear in certain sectors that Mrs Fitzherbert was part of a popish plot to introduce Catholics into Parliament. Articles appeared in newspapers and pamphlets that criticised the Prince and Mrs Fitzherbert, and on several occasions writs were brought against authors and sellers alike, as in this case recorded in *The Times* of 29 April 1786:

We hear the report is true, that Mr Fores, the printseller in Piccadilly, has a prosecution commenced against him for selling a print supposed to allude to the Prince of Wales and Mrs Fitzherbert. Justice Hyde served a warrant upon him on Monday. … The prosecution is supposed to commence from Carleton House [home of the Prince of Wales], as Mr Weltje [Louis Weltje, the Prince's maitre d'hôtel] has the entire direction, the justices refusing and delaying to take any steps till he came to the office.

Attacks on the press continued, some with far more sinister overtones than the mere prosecution case above, as here in an article entitled 'Another Attack on the Liberty of the Press':

On Wednesday last, Charles Smith Esq., brother to Mrs Fitzherbert … called on Mr Walter, in Piccadilly, after having visited the Office in Printing House Square in Blackfriars, for the purpose of knowing whether he as the Editor of *The Times?* The question seeming to command, rather than solicit an answer, Mr Walter replied, 'that it was not usual to satisfy such interrogatories'. Mr. Smith, on this, announced himself to be the brother of Mrs Fitzherbert, and having mentioned that he saw many scurrilous matters respecting that Lady in *The Times*, declared in an authoritative tone, that if the paper should Dare in future, to mention one disagreeable or disrespectful word of his sister, or even so much as her name, he would Punish him as Editor for so doing. … Mr Walter opened the door of the closet, in which this conversation was held, that two Gentlemen in the adjacent parlour might witness what was said, when there was a repetition of the threats in a very menacing tone of voice. Whether this kind of bravado conduct in Mr Smith, will have any influence on the spirited truths sent to *The Times* for publication, either respecting Mrs Fitzherbert, or any other public character, its future conduct will shew. – At present we shall only say that we are not to be TERRIFIED.

(*The Times*, 6 February 1789)

But yet the questions were still being asked. When the politician Fox openly refuted the rumours that the marriage had taken place, it was reported in the press that:

Mr Sheridan owes the respect paid to him, at present, both by the Prince and Mrs Fitzherbert, to the ingenuity with which he destroyed the effect of Mr Fox's declaration in the House of Commons – 'that the Prince and Mrs F were not married'. Mr Sheridan, at that time, paid a very handsome compliment to Mrs Fitzherbert's virtue! And what other inference could the public draw from such a compliment, than that she was actually the Princess of Wales?

(*The Times*, 24 January 1789)

These attacks and questions about their situation put a strain on their relationship and it was not too long before the Prince was casting his eye elsewhere. A brief interlude occurred with the singer Mrs Crouch before he fell madly in love (yet again) with the Lady Jersey. He paid off Mrs Fitzherbert with an annuity of £3,000 and she sold up her home in London and moved to Margate.

Lady Jersey was as dissolute as the Prince himself, but she was also scheming and self-seeking. Persuading the Prince that, without Mrs Fitzherbert, he was now free to marry a Protestant princess and also to increase his income by so doing, she suggested he should marry his cousin, Princess Caroline of Brunswick. This was a decision that pleased the King very much and he consented. George and Caroline were duly married on 8 April 1795. At this time Lady Jersey was installed as Lady of the Bed Chamber and she took every opportunity of humiliating the Princess whenever she could. Caroline would not stand for this and demanded that she be removed from that position. By the end of 1796, Lady Jersey had resigned from the position. That year was a busy one for the Prince, he had broken off his affair with Lady Jersey and also requested a formal separation from the Princess; things had not been going well, even though their daughter Charlotte had been born earlier in the year. Although he briefly was reconciled with Mrs Fitzherbert, he cast his eye about again and this time it rested on Isabella Anne Seymour-Conway, the Marchioness of Hertford.

Isabella had been born Isabella Anne Frances Ingram, the daughter of Charles Ingram, the Viscount Irwin. Born at Temple Newsam in 1759, she was only sixteen years old when she was married to Francis Seymour-Conway, the 2nd Marquis of Hertford. For him it was his second marriage, his first wife having died. Thrust into the world of the aristocracy at a relatively young age, Isabella now found herself to be a very wealthy and influential lady. Not only was she co-heiress to the Temple Newsam estate with her other siblings (there were five girls in the family and no boys), she was now the mistress of properties in Worcestershire, Norfolk, Ireland and London. She rapidly became one of the 'fashionables' that the newspapers of the time alluded to. Tall and willowy as a young woman, it is hardly surprising that she attracted the attention of the Prince. When and how they met is not exactly known but it is likely to have been at a ball or concert in Manchester House in London, the city home of the Hertfords. The Prince was also quite close to their wayward son, Lord Yarmouth. Perhaps he saw a kindred spirit in him, as he was also known for being a wastrel and a drunkard, although he was apparently good at cricket. Lord Yarmouth married the wealthy heiress Maria Fagnani. For him it was a marriage of convenience and it was frowned upon by his parents. He soon became estranged from them and moved with his wife to Paris. It was the Prince who sought to reunite son and parents and, when the Treaty of Amiens broke down in 1803 and British nationals were held in France, it was the Prince who successfully lobbied Charles Fox to negotiate his release in 1806.

The initial rejections of the Prince's advances towards Isabella caused him to fall into his customary state of self-pity and melancholy. When visiting Doncaster races in the autumn of 1806, he was in such a pitiable state that only a visit to Isabella at Temple Newsam would cheer him, especially as her husband was away on business in Ireland at the time. Under the vaguely disguised premise of visiting the Dowager Lady Irwin, the Prince and his brother spent three days there. *The Newcastle Courant* gives a brief mention of the visit on 11 October 1806:

On Monday se'ennight [week] His Royal Highness the Prince of Wales, honoured Lady Irwin, at Temple Newsham [*sic*], with a visit; and on Tuesday hunted with Lord Darlington [possibly at Raby Castle, near Staindrop]. On Wednesday His Royal Highness and the Duke of Clarence [his brother] paid a visit to the Archbishop of York, at Bishopthorp, after which they returned to Ledstone, whence they set off for on Thursday London, and arrived there on Sunday.

He enjoyed his brief stay at Temple Newsam so much that he gave Isabella a gift of delicate hand-painted Chinese wallpaper as a token of his affection. It was not until a few years later, about 1820, that Isabella got around to mounting the wallpaper in what is known as the Chinese Drawing Room, also sometime referred to as the Blue Room. It was obviously not decorative enough for her as she decided to embellish the paper with pasted-on bird cut-outs. She had recently received a copy of Audubon's book *The Birds of America*, containing many hand-painted illustrations of birds. She 'vandalised' her copy, although she would not have considered this so, by cutting out many of the illustrations, and had them pasted directly onto the wallpaper. Careful conservation has preserved the paper in situ and it can still be seen today. Audubon's book is now rare and had it been left intact it would be valued in the region of £7.5 million pounds today. In hindsight we might consider it to have been something of an expensive decoration project for Isabella. The wallpaper was not the only gift the Prince bestowed on her during their relationship. Later, in 1818, *The Chester Chronicle* reported:

> The Prince Regent has presented his beautiful Shetland pony, and a superb garden Phaeton [a light four-wheeled carriage] to the Marchioness of Hertford!
>
> (28 August 1818)

It was also earlier in 1806 that the Marquis and Marchioness of Hertford became embroiled in the 'Minney Seymour Guardianship Case'. Although the Prince and Mrs Fitzherbert did not have children together, in 1801 Mrs Fitzherbert had taken temporary guardianship of the infant child Mary 'Minney' Seymour while her father, Lord Hugh Seymour, pursued a naval career and his wife was convalescing from an illness in Madeira. Sadly, later that year, both parents died and there was a question as to where Minney should be placed. Lord Hugh's executors were concerned that, amongst other things, the Protestant child was being brought up in a Catholic household. There was much debate, resulting in the decision that Minney should remain with Mrs Fitzherbert on a temporary basis. The Prince, adoring the child and wishing her to be a companion for his own daughter Charlotte, proposed himself to stand as guardian. This was rejected, and the Earl of Euston and Lord Henry Seymour were appointed joint guardians. The Prince took the matter to a higher court but was rejected there as well. His case finally went before the House of Lords in 1806, and was reported on at length by *The Morning Post* on 16 June 1806. After many speeches from representatives of both parties, the Lords decreed four resolutions:

> First, That so much of the decree that goes to authorise the appointment of the Earl of Euston, and Lord Henry Seymour, as Guardians of the Appellant, be reversed.
>
> Second, That so much of the said decree, as dismissed the petition of the Appellant, praying for the appointment of Maria Fitzherbert as her Guardian, be adirmed [approved].
>
> Third, That so much of the said decree that authorises the appointment of the Marquis of Hertford as Guardian, be reversed.

Fourth, This resolution was of some length, and in some degree appeared to modify the effect of the third. It appeared in substance to be – that, inasmuch as the Marquis of Hertford, nearest in blood to the Appellant, and the Marchioness of Hertford, seemed willing to become Guardians to the Appellant, it is ordered, under the particular circumstances of the case, that the said Marquis and Marchioness of Hertford be appointed Guardians.

The Prince was pleased with the outcome, especially when it was agreed that Minney should stay within the custody of Mrs Fitzherbert, with the Hertfords as the legal guardians. The Marquis stated:

As far as his knowledge and observation went, the health, morals, education and, above all, instruction in the Protestant religion, were most carefully attended to, declared, that in accepting the Guardianship of his niece, he would enter into no promise or stipulation whatever, as to his future conduct respecting her. – He should use his own discretion, either in suffering her to remain in her present situation, or removing her from it, as he should deem most conducive to her comfort, happiness and advantage.

The matter only ingratiated the Marchioness more in the Prince's esteem, and after his visit to her later that year, he became infatuated with her. When he was away from her he was doleful and melancholic and he began to look ill, so much so that some people feared for his health; others saw his condition as being self-induced and a melodramatic sham to lure Isabella to him. As his condition appeared to worsen, the Hertfords relented and travelled to London to see him. He was miraculously cured by her presence and she became his bosom companion from that time on.

The nature of their affair has long been debated. At the time that they had begun their association Isabella was almost fifty years old and the Prince in his mid-forties. Was it a sexual relationship or purely platonic? Like many of his mistresses, Isabella was older than the Prince. Some have conjectured that George had had issues with his mother as a child and therefore sought the company of older women; women who would dote on him and mother him. Whatever their relationship may have been, the Prince confided in her and she became very influential in his politics and affairs of state. It also meant that her husband was granted favours. In 1804, he was Master of the Horse, and in 1807, he was invested as a Knight of the Garter. He was later made Lord Chamberlain of the Household. There appears to have been some advantages of being the husband of a royal mistress!

In October 1807, Lady Irwin became ill and the family gathered at Temple Newsam. Four of the five sisters were present.

> The Marchioness of Hertford is now bestowing that dutiful attention on her venerable mother, Lady Irwin, at Temple Newsam in Yorkshire, for which filial piety Lady Hertford has been so much distinguished. … Lady William Gordon [Frances] and Miss Gordon, Mr and Mrs Meynell [Elizabeth], Mrs Harvey Aston [Harriet], &c. are at present inmates at Temple Newsam.
>
> (*The Morning Post*, 27 October 1807)

Only Louisa, Mrs Ramsden Barone, was not mentioned, and therefore we assume she was not present at the family gathering. Although it seems that Lady Irwin was making a slight recovery at the time of the above report, she passed away on Friday, 23 October.

> DIED: On Friday morning, aged 74, the Right Hon. Viscountess Irwin, of Temple Newsom [*sic*] in Yorkshire. Lady Irwin was mother to the Marchioness of Hertford, Lady William Gordon, and Mrs Meynell, relict of Mr Meynell, of Hoare-Cross, Staffordshire. By the death of this lady, Mr Meynell, her grandson [Hugo Charles Meynell], who is just of age, will succeed to very large estates in Sussex and Yorkshire. Her Ladyship died very rich.
>
> (*Northampton Mercury*, 23 October 1807)

The above report was not entirely accurate. The estate of the Irwin family descended first to Isabella and Frances, as co-heirs, but Isabella maintained control of the properties. In December, after the death of the Dowager Lady

Irwin, the King granted the Hertfords the right to include the name Ingram in their family. The *Kentish Gazette* of 29 December records this:

> The King has been graciously pleased to give and grant unto the most honourable Francis Seymour Conway Marquis of Hertford [and his wife the Marchioness] … his royal licence and authority, that they may … take and use the name of Ingram before their present surnames of Seymour and Conway, and also write the said surname of Ingram before all titles of honour.

After the death of her mother, the Prince wrote and begged Isabella to return to London. At first she did not respond, sending him once more into a fit of depression, before she returned after a suitable period of mourning. Once more, the Prince began to recuperate in her company, much to the distaste of both his wife, Princess Caroline, and his former mistress, Mrs Fitzherbert. Isabella took the opportunity whenever she could to humiliate Mrs Fitzherbert. It was a calculated move. Aware that the press were closely observing her and the Prince, she made sure that when she visited the Prince, Mrs Fitzherbert was also present. In this way, Mrs Fitzherbert suffered the indignity of witnessing her rival being publicly acknowledged, whilst Isabella retained her reputation. By 1811, the Prince had formally separated from Mrs Fitzherbert, and Isabella was the centre of his attention.

The year 1811 also saw the decline of the King's health; further bouts of 'madness' had set in and he was not able to fulfil his role. It has long been thought that the King suffered from acute intermittent porphyria (AIP). This is a chemical imbalance within the body that can cause neurological problems and episodes of irrational behaviour. One of the symptoms of AIP is the blue colouration of urine in the sufferer, something the King presented with at these times. However, there is evidence to show that this discolouration may have been due to medicine he was given based on the gentian plant. Others claim he may have been suffering from some form of psychiatric illness, such as bipolar disorder or manic–depressive psychosis. The historian Lucy Worsley refers to this in an article for the online BBC Magazine of 15 April 2013. If this is the case, and of course retrospective diagnosis is often just conjecture, then it might go some way to explain Prince George's own phases of mania and depression.

Due to the incapacity of the King, Parliament initially granted the Prince a period of 'restricted regency' in early 1811, in which he had all the power of the monarch, except in name. When the King failed to respond to treatment, and it was clear that he would not recover, the Prince then moved to 'unrestricted regency' the following year. He was now referred to as the Prince Regent and this ushered in what we now know as the Regency period.

Isabella was now a wealthy member of high society; the 'fashionables'. During 'the season', many were the assemblies, balls, concerts and routs (a large party or social gathering) given at Manchester House, sometimes now referred to as Hertford House. The Prince, other members of the royal family and visiting nobility were often present. These affairs were grand and lavish, with sometimes upwards of 500 'fashionables' present. The press were expansive in the descriptions of these events:

THE MARCHIONESS OF HERTFORD'S ROUT
On Tuesday evening, in Manchester-square, Hertford House was illuminated in a style of the most refulgent splendour, in compliment to the Grand Duke Michael of Russia. The seven apartments on the ground floor, with all their matchless embellishments, were thrown open at ten o'clock. An additional object of attraction was the garden, which was also lighted up with many thousand variegated lamps, interspersed among the trees in a variety of beautiful forms. ... In the interior of the mansion, a temporary conservatory was formed. The agreeable odour of the plants, and the coolness of the rooms, were delightful. ... The most costly refreshments were provided, set out on tables in the saloon, with indescribable taste and grandeur.

(*The Morning Post*, 9 July 1818)

Top of the guest list was, of course, the now Prince Regent, and the article goes on to list several other princes, ambassadors, dukes and duchesses, marquises and marchionesses, earls and countesses, lords, ladies and knights. Also listed are a lower order of military officers, messrs, mistresses and misses. A small number of foreign counts conclude the list. It really was a glittering occasion, and this would have been only one of many throughout the fashionable season. It was a case of an excuse for a celebration. When the Prince hosted a visit to London by victorious allies in 1814, the houses of the fashionables were decorated to a high degree. *The Norfolk Chronicle* of 16 April 1814 describes:

> The residence of the Marquis of Hertford displayed considerable taste. The portico and veranda were ornamented with the Bourbon Lilies, and other emblems, and 'Vivent les Bourbons'.

Isabella was now at the height of society. Although approaching fifty years of age, she was always elegant, well dressed and coiffeured. Her dresses were often commented upon in the press, especially during the 1813 season, and were of great interest to female readers. This from *The Morning Post*, 8 February 1813, describes her at the Prince Regent's Ball and Supper:

> The company were then all standing around the room. The ladies were attired mostly in white silks, ornamented with the most exquisitely wrought lace of the same colour; those worn by the Marchioness of Hertford … were really most unique. The female head-dress was … a-la-grecque, with a plume of ostrich feathers, introduced solely in compliment to the Regent's crest.

And from the *Kentish Gazette* of the next day, the Marchioness of Hertford wore 'a most magnificent white satin dress, ornamented with gold'.

At the marriage celebrations of Princess Charlotte of Wales, the Prince Regent's daughter, Isabella was described as wearing:

> [the costume] of the Marchioness of Hertford is of an immense size, the sleeves are short and full, with plaiting, or rather ruffles, of French blond at the bottom. The lappets, and those points where lace can be introduced, are to be French blond; the head-dress, bands of diamonds, and immense plumes of ostrich feathers.
>
> (*Kentish Weekly News*, 12 April 1816)

And in May, she wore:

> a petticoat of rich white satin, with net draperies, most beautifully embroidered in silver lama, and blue floss silk, forming borders, peculiar for their richness and elegance of effect. The draperies tastefully looped with a beautiful silver cord and tassels. The whole finished at the bottom with a handsome garniture of net in roses. Train of sapphire blue satin, profusely and elegantly trimmed with silver and blond lama. Head-dress, rich ostrich plume, with most superb bobbinets.
>
> (*Bell's Weekly Messenger*, 19 May 1816)

The Marchioness must have cut quite a stunning figure at these events, so much so that she appeared that year in the August edition of *The Lady's Monthly Museum*. This was a monthly publication aimed at the female reader and usually included a portrait of an eminent lady of society, sketches and tinted plates of the finest morning and evening wear for the month, as well as biographies, stories and interesting essays. To appear in this would be like being featured in *Vogue* or *Harper's Bazaar* today.

> *THE LADY'S MONTHLY MUSEUM* – on the 1st of August was published, price 1s 6d, embellished with a most exquisite likeness of the Marchioness of Hertford.
>
> (*The Courier*, 19 August 1816)

Isabella, and her husband, the Marquis, were firm supporters of Tory policies. They believed in the authority of the monarchy, the hierarchical values of the aristocracy, and they were staunchly Protestant. The Catholic Emancipation Bill was anathema to them and they were strongly against it. Before his affair with the Marchioness, the Prince had generally favoured the policies of the Whigs. Charles Fox, the eminent Whig politician, was a close friend and looked to the Prince for support. The Prince, perhaps because of his attachment to Mrs Fitzherbert, leaned towards Catholic emancipation. However, once he had turned his back on her and embraced (perhaps quite literally) the Marchioness of Hertford, his views began to change. There was no doubt that Isabella was having an influence on the

Prince and matters of state, particularly when he became regent. He broke with the Whigs and elected to keep the Tories in power under Spencer Perceval. The Marchioness was seen as being behind all of this. She was criticised in the House of Lords. Lord Grey referred to her as 'an unseen and separate influence which lurked behind the throne' (M.J. Levy, 1966). The press began to ask questions about her influence:

> *The Times* asks, and seriously too, of what consequence it is to the country, whether the Marchioness of Hertford ... undertakes the management of the state? ... We answer that the situation of the Prince Regent is now very different from what it was during the actual government of his father ... for the Prince had then nothing to do with it. The case now however is far otherwise, and the people of England have too much love and respect for His Royal Highness to fancy that he stands in need of any female counsellor. ... This confession of the primary cause of the Prince's present attachment to Tory politics must be rather humiliating to Mr Perceval and Lord Castlereagh, who it seems, owe their exalted situations not to their own public talents, but to the private friendship of a fair politician.
>
> (*The Oxford University and City Herald*, 21 March 1812)

The Examiner of 29 March was far more satirical in its approach to the matter, leading off with: 'It is notorious that the Prince Regent pays constant visits at the residence of the Marchioness of Hertford, in Manchester-square.'

The paper went on to carry two 'letters' that certainly poked fun at the situation, the first a little tongue in cheek and the second downright comical, both at the expense of the Prince and the Marchioness of Hertford:

> Mr Examiner – I live at a village at a distance from the metropolis, where I, with a few honest neighbours meet every Tuesday evening, to read your paper. ... Earl Grey ... said there was a secret and destructive influence behind the throne, which would prove the ruin of the empire. We are at a loss as to guess what it could be. ... We suppose it must be something supernatural – some magician or sorceress – for it is the general opinion in this part of the country that the Regent is bewitched.

… Whatever this something may be, we ought not to rest till it is dragged to public view.

Mr Examiner – I have just received your paper of last Sunday, from which a man might be led to imagine that His Royal Highness the Prince Regent has totally abandoned the Wigs [*sic*]. As an intimate friend of the peruke-maker [wig maker] to His Royal Highness, I beg leave to assure you, that the report is entirely without foundation. So far from an abandonment of Wigs by His Royal Highness I can most positively assert, that wears not only one but four at a time! This may appear strange to common minds, Mr Examiner, but it is no more strange than true, as my friend the peruke-maker to His Royal Highness can well vouch. One wig is clapped on the right side; one wig on the left side; one wig behind; and one wig before; forming the Grande juvenile curl. – If any of your readers, Mr Examiner, should doubt my veracity, let them but apply to my friend the perruqier, and they will find it to be Gospel.

It was not long before satirical prints were being produced for sale by the likes of George Cruikshank and others. Some of them had blatant sexual innuendo, such as the one titled *The Hertford Doctoress*. In this a rather portly Marchioness is attending to the big toe of the Prince, his foot resting in her lap. He is saying, 'I wish this seat of mine was like a music stool that I might screw it up or down at pleasure. Oh, my dear, mind how you touch it for it is very tender, altho' it is not so large as it was by a great deal.'

She replies, 'I shall be very gentle with it my Love, but I think the application I am going to put to it will do it good, as you say, it is certainly not so big as it was: but I think it has swell'd a little since it has been in my lap.'

Meanwhile, the Princess Caroline is peering at them from behind a door. Her speech bubble begins, 'Hertford air indeed!! Might as well send him to Jersey [reference to his former mistress Lady Jersey].'

These were all widely circulated and the general public found them highly amusing. The implication from some of them was that their affair did indeed have sexual overtones. Another print is titled *R***l Hobbys*, and this one is even more blatantly suggestive. The image shows the well-endowed

Marchioness riding stride-legs across the body of the obese Prince, as if he was a 'hobby' – what we would today term a balance bike. She wears a coronet and carries a whip in her hand, while saying to the Prince, 'Come up you idle fellow. I'll make you Drive it Home! – you shall remember pushing your Hobby in Hertford!!!' Prince Frederick is shown in the background, riding his own hobby as the Prince says to him, 'Oh dear Fred, this is tight work for a P – e of my constitution. I do not think I shall be able to Push it Home.' Again, the innuendo is quite clear and one wonders how both the Prince and the Marchioness reacted to such brazen caricatures.

Not all publications were against them. By contrast, *The London Courier* of 25 March 1812 takes a different attitude towards Isabella, lending support to the Tory government:

> In what way is the charge of favouritism applicable to the present Cabinet? … Perhaps the reproach of favouritism is intended, not against Ministers, but against private persons, against the Marchioness of Hertford, whose influence over the Regent is said to be great. Lord Grey resorts to the hacknied cant of 'something behind the throne greater than the throne itself', thus countenancing … the scandal with which the Journals of his party teem … but taking it for granted that the Marchioness of Hertford does influence, by her advice, the conduct of the Regent – what then? … but if we are to consider the conduct of affairs as a result of the Marchioness of Hertford's advice, we shall most sincerely pray her as Britain's guardian angel. If it be that Lady who has persuaded the Regent to continue in power … and to conduct himself so dutifully as a Son, so patriotically as a Prince, we hope to hear of His Royal Highness's visits at Manchester-square every day in the week.

All of George's relationships were doomed to failure. His affair with Isabella was no different. During their relationship he had experienced both personal joy and despair. He had seen his daughter Charlotte marry in 1816 and then die the following year. His mother then died in November 1818. To the needy and insecure Prince, all of this must have been a bitter blow. He was growing older and Isabella was now a grandmother approaching sixty years of age. She had supported him, advised him and comforted him for more than thirteen years, but his eye was beginning to wander yet again. This time it settled on Lady Conyngham, and in December 1819 he formally broke with the Marchioness of Hertford. Had she remained with the Prince just a little longer, she would have found herself to be the mistress of a king. Sadly for her, the old King George died in January 1820, just one month after her break-up with the Prince. Who knows what would have been in store for her if they had stayed together.

She maintained her London life and often returned to the country seat at Temple Newsam. After the Marquis of Hertford died in 1822, she spent 'the season' in London but always returned to Temple Newsam at other times. Much of her time in Leeds was spent in charitable works within the county. In 1825, she donated ten guineas for the relief of widows, orphans and relatives of those killed in the explosion at Middleton Colliery. The Marchioness was patron or subscriber of many events and societies: the York Bazaar for the relief of the distressed manufacturers; the Pontefract Dispensary Bazaar; the Lying-in Hospital Bazaar; the County Hospital; the Yorkshire Institution for the Deaf; the West Riding Medical Charitable Society; the Benevolent, or Strangers' Friend Society; and the Relief of the Poor of Rothwell – to name but a few. It is little wonder that *The Leeds Intelligencer* of 17 August 1826 states that her 'benevolent liberality to the poor is subject to constant and deserved eulogy'.

And an excellent example of her work was given by the same newspaper on 3 January 1833:

According to good custom of long standing, the benevolence of the Marchioness of Hertford has this season been dispensed to the poor around Temple-Newsam. A few days ago her Ladyship caused two fine fat bullocks to be distributed; broken victuals, soup, &c. are dispensed twice a week; and many indigent persons have been supplied with warm clothing. On Monday evening, the servants, with the sanction of the noble Marchioness, gave their annual ball and supper. It is scarcely necessary to say that the best the mansion afforded was entirely at their command.

The world was changing rapidly and, during the latter years of her life, the Marchioness had to accept that canals, the new railways and roads were all to encroach upon her estate, at an agreed price, it must be said. The West Yorkshire Joint Services has a collection of legal documents relating to dealings between the Marchioness, or her representatives, and representatives of the Aire & Calder Navigation, the Leeds to Selby Railway and the Leeds to Selby Turnpike. She even had to accept that a twenty-two-year lease had been agreed for the extraction of coal from certain areas of the estate. As she neared the end of her eventful life, Temple Newsam was no longer to be the tranquil home of her childhood. *The Leeds Intelligencer* of 19 April 1834 gave the report of her death:

> We regret to announce the death of this venerable and generous-hearted lady; it took place in London, on Saturday evening, after a short illness, occasioned, we understand, by a cold while on her way from Temple-Newsam to her town residence, about a fortnight previously. It is stated that, while on the journey, the wheel of her Ladyship's carriage took fire from friction, and that she alighted at a small inn on the road-side, and she was shewn into a room without fire, the sudden chill of which occasioned cold, and led, as we have observed, to a fatal result. ... The extensive property inherited by the deceased marchioness from her father ... descends ... to Hugo Meynell Esq. eldest son of Mrs Meynell, the third daughter of the late Viscount Irvine [Frances, Lady William Gordon, the second daughter, had no children]. ... Of the departed Marchioness it is scarcely possible to speak in sufficiently strong words of praise. Her intellectual character, and high attainments, formed the least part of her excellencies; however enlightened her mind, her heart was warmer still. To the poor and the distressed her munificence was all but unbounded ... many thousands a-year did she regularly thus distribute in the most unostentatious manner; her charity, indeed, was of that genuine kind which anxiously courts concealment; the right hand hardly knowing what the left hand did. In her political predilections the Noble Marchioness was warmly Tory, yet zealous for the rights, liberties and welfare of the people.

For all the good and charitable works that Isabella may have done, it is as one of the mistresses of the Prince of Wales, later George IV, that she will long be remembered.

Chapter 7

A Hidden House

The 'unseen' workers within the house: the servants

Every historic building has a story to tell and that story is frequently told from the owners' point of view; their histories are very often recorded in detail. The lords, ladies, knights and other titled gentry who have owned Temple Newsam are only a part of the story. As you stroll through the ornately furnished rooms it is sometimes easy to forget that there were other, far more important, inhabitants of the house – the servants and estate workers. Occasionally you are allowed to take a tour of the hidden areas of Temple Newsam: the back stairs, cellars and other areas that the servants frequented. Those who worked there were like an invisible army of ants, ensuring that the business of the house was kept in order on a daily basis. Servants were rarely to be seen, only out of necessity, and theirs was a nether world of stone staircases, dark passageways and damp cellars.

The stone steps of the servants' staircase are worn from the countless number of feet that have run up and down them over the years. Beneath the courtyard runs a narrow diagonal subterranean passage, linking the south and north wings. It was built in the early eighteenth century to link the original kitchen area in the south wing to the rest of the house. Here, servants – some as young as maybe twelve years old – would have scurried around carrying all sorts of things. Today, the eerie passage is lit by low-light electric bulbs but in earlier times it would have been unlit, damp, cold, and possibly vermin-ridden. The kitchens were relocated to the north wing by the Marchioness of Hertford during the 1790s, and servants' passages were later added so that they had access to areas of the house without always having to use the underground passage.

The former kitchen space was turned into a 'brushing room', where the owners and their guests would enter after a day of hunting, remove their muddy boots and be 'brushed down' by servants before retiring upstairs. A red baize door in the cellar leads to a stone stairway where servants would carry cooked food from the kitchens to the serving room. This was where food was kept warm until it was served in the adjacent dining room. The largely original Tudor cellars are a labyrinth of connected rooms, now mainly used for storage. One of the most important of these would have been the wine cellar, kept behind a locked door, and only the steward or butler would have been the key-holder. This would have contained some of the more expensive 'food' items of the house, and the contents were often quite extensive. An inventory of the wine cellar from 1871 shows that it held:

    3,800 gallons of ale, 110 gallons of beer
    96 bottles Champagne & 36 pint bottles Champagne
    474 bottles Sherry & 5 bottles Manzanilla (Sherry) & 48 bottles
        Amontillado (Sherry)
    136 bottles light Claret & 32 pint bottles Claret
    72 bottles fine Claret
    144 bottles Chateau Lafitte (Claret)
    32 bottles Sauternes
    93 bottles Hock
    30 bottles Moselle
    34 bottles Carlowitz [Hungarian wine]
    16 bottles Madeira & 62 bottles East India Madeira
    154 bottles Port & 52 bottles old Port
    60 bottles Marsala
    7 bottles of spirits and liquours [unspecified]
                                                (Temple Newsam collection)

It is little wonder that such an extensive wine cellar was held under lock and key! The butler or steward was an important member of the household staff; if the lords and ladies of the house were the 'officers', then he certainly was the 'regimental sergeant major', and ruled below stairs. Amongst other things, he would detail the weekly expenditure and keep meticulous records, as in this instance for the week 5 April 1799 (WYL100/WEA/14/16 WYAS):

Aerial view of Temple Newsam House, post-1980. (*Photographer unknown; author's collection*)

View looking across the middle and lower lakes. (*Author's photograph*)

The Little Temple as it is today. (*Reproduced by permission of Richard Thomson*)

The Stable Block viewed from the House. (*Author's photograph*)

Home Farm viewed from the visitor entrance. (*Author's photograph*)

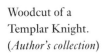

Domesday Book entry for Neuhusū. (*The National Archives*)

Woodcut of a
Templar Knight.
(*Author's collection*)

Templar Cross on
a Whitkirk cottage.
(*Author's photograph*)

Darcy Coat of Arms. (*The General Armory of England, Scotland, Ireland & Wales, Harrison & sons., London, 1884*)

The Banner of the Holy Wounds. (*Mod. Diego Sanguinetti*)

Blue plaque commemorating the rising of the Pilgrimage of Grace in Louth, Lincolnshire. (*Author's photograph*)

Henry VIII, from the workshop of Hans Holbein the Younger. (*Walker Gallery*)

Mary Queen of Scots, engraving by Alexander Ritchie, 1852. (*Library of Congress*)

Lord Darnley, King of Scotland. (*Universal Magazine of Knowledge and Pleasure, 1749*)

James I, engraving by Van der Gucht, c.1700. (*Library of Congress*)

Portrait of Ludovic Stewart, 2nd Duke of Lennox, by Simon van de Passe. (*British Museum*)

The Darnley Room. (*Illustrated London News, 1885*)

Queen Elizabeth I, three portraits, c.1901: youth, middle age, and old age. (*Library of Congress*)

A Civil War skirmish re-enacted by The Sealed Knot. (*Author's photograph*)

Typical courtyard structure of a Tudor house: Cadhay House, Ottery St Mary, Devon. (*Reproduced by permission of Derek Voller*)

J. Kip engraving of Temple Newsam, c.1699. (*Reproduced by permission of Heritage Technology Ltd., 2007*)

3D image of Temple Newsam House based on the Kip engraving. (*Reproduced by permission of Heritage Technology Ltd., 2007*)

Lancelot 'Capability' Brown, by Nathaniel Dance, c.1773. (*Original painting in the National Portrait Gallery*)

The Avenue, leading from the House to the eastern gate on Bullerthorpe Lane. (*Reproduced by permission of Lis Burke*)

The Sphynx Gates. (*Author's photograph*)

The Prince Regent, by John Russell, c.1792.
(*Library of Congress*)

The Marchioness of Hertford, Isabella
Seymour-Conway; mezzotint by James Scott.
(*Pub. Henry Graves & Co., 1868*)

Indigo Bird – an illustration from J.J. Audubon.
(*Library of Congress*)

Engraving of Temple Newsam, c. 1820. (*Author's collection*)

The Learned Ladies, Tinderbox Theatre production at Temple Newsam. (*Author's photograph*)

Monstrosities of 1818; satirical print by George Cruikshank. (*Library of Congress*)

The Servant, by Frederic R. Gruger, c.1900. (*Library of Congress*)

A stable yard scene, by Charles M. Relyea, c.1900. (*Library of Congress*)

A gamekeeper on his
rounds: *The Warrener*, by
George Morland, c.1900.
(*Library of Congress*)

Bailiff's truncheon.
(*Author's photograph*)

Temple Newsam,
woodblock print, c.1880.
(*Pub. William McKenzie,
London*)

The visit of the Duke and Duchess of York. (*Illustrated London News, 1894*)

The Blue Lady? (*Reproduced by permission of David Pacey*)

Postcard of Temple Newsam, c.1914. (*Author's collection*)

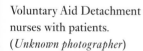

Voluntary Aid Detachment
nurses with patients.
(*Unknown photographer*)

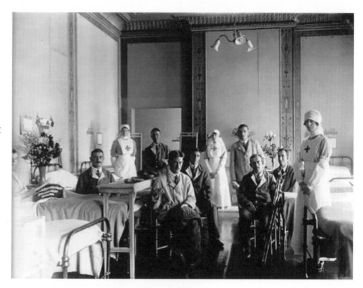

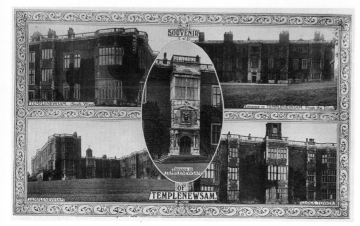

Souvenir postcard of
Temple Newsam, c.1920.
(*Unknown photographer,
author's collection*)

Temple Newsam tram terminus, 1950s. (*Reproduced by permission of Neil Clifton*)

An afternoon rehearsal by Tinderbox Theatre in the amphitheatre. (*Author's photograph*)

Opera in the Park. (*Reproduced by permission of Richard Thomson*)

	£	s	d
Veale 3lb	1	1	6
Lamb		6	6
2 Calves heads		3	2
8 Calves feet		1	2
6 Salmon		13	0
Codds heads		4	8
1 Doz. Lemons and Oranges		3	9
9 Fowls		15	0
Hund. Oysters		5	0
Peck Apples		9	0
18lb Butter		18	0
8 (?) Cream		8	0
5 Salmon		10	0
Codds		4	4
Cheese		7	8
11 Score eggs		9	8
8 Fowls		12	0
2 Chimneys swept		2	0
15lb Butter		15	0
Charwoman		1	6
Veale		18	3
3 Sweetbreads		2	0
Turnpikes and expenses		3	0

He would also record who came and went in the household, as the record goes on to show:

18 [April]   Lord & Lady Heartford [sic] came and left 18 for London
19 [April]   Lady Wm & Miss Gordon set off for London

The 'lower' servants, those who were never seen, would have taken their meals in the cellar complex. Here there were strict rules: no swearing, no dirt and no rude behaviour. The butler would have eaten upstairs in his

Butler's Pantry, or perhaps with more senior servants in an upstairs room, although still 'below stairs' in relation to the owners.

Although the servants busied away like ants in a nest, making sure that everything ran like clockwork, they are seldom recorded by name. Their histories are not written but snippets of information can be gleaned about them from records kept in archives. Amongst the Temple Newsam collection held by the West Yorkshire Archives is a folder of receipts for wages and other expenses (WYL100/EA/12/19). Dating back to the seventeenth century, here can be found some of the names of those 'below stairs' and, perhaps more interestingly, how much they earned. Most of the wages would have actually been paid by the steward on behalf of the master of the house.

Servants tended to be paid half-yearly; on Lady Day, 25 March, or at Michaelmas, 25 September. However, this was not always so and many servants went for quite a while before actually receiving their wages in their hands. In 1701 there is a receipt from Anne Jordan for the sum of £4 13s (approximately £365 today) in respect of 'for 2 years + ¼ + 3 weeks' wages now due to me at my going away'. Her wage, which would have included board and lodging, was quite low and would have reflected her status when compared to the amount received by John Loads only a few years earlier in 1682. He receipted the sum of £17, 'one half year's salary for keeping and training light horses for the daughter of my Lord Ingram'. This half year sum equates to approximately £1,500 today. Put in comparative terms, poor Anne received 9½d per week for her services whereas John earned 13s per week. One of the lengthiest wait for actual wages was receipted by a Luke Turner. He eventually received £50 'for wages paid ½ yearly between Michaelmas 1651 and Michaelmas 1655 at £5 a half year'. This wait compares markedly with money received by Thos. Howard in 1715: '£1 – 1s – 6d for 14 days' wages, being a cook at Temple Newsam'.

Sometimes, as in some of the above, not only are the servants named but also the service they have given. In 1702, a Reverend Hutton received £15 for being the Chaplain to his Lordship. A little earlier, a Mr Roebuck received from Lady Irwin the sum of £4 for 'my wife's nursing of Sir Arthur Ingram'. From 1700 to 1730, John Grolsch received £10 for looking after the gardens, and Peter Wilson received 15s for horse breaking. M. Goodall made his mark, receiving £3 for a half year's wages and 5s for 'a frock agreed by me'.

The receipts in the collection are not only for servants within the house. There is an interesting set of figures from 1692 that details female labour in the fields:

To the women for making hay and moving it in stacks		August 1692
Wade wife that died	16 days	0 – 8 – 0
Widd. [widow] Smith	13 days	0 – 6 – 6
Barnby wife	21 days	0 – 10 – 6
Wilcock Xchstne [Christine?]	24½ days	0 – 12 – 3
R. Cunnif wife	19½	0 – 9 – 9
Walker wife	18	0 – 9 – 0
her daughter	1 day	0 – 0 – 3
Clough wife	16 days	0 – 8 – 0
Old Hardy	22 days	0 – 11 – 0
Ann Harrison	23	0 – 11 – 6
Ann Hardwick	23½	0 – 11 – 9
Atkinson wife	19	0 – 9 – 6
her sister Bettrix	19½	0 – 9 – 9
Deborah	26	0 – 13 – 0
Mary Turton	25	0 – 12 – 6
Sar. Fenton	21½	0 – 10 – 9
Susana Hardwick	30½	0 – 15 – 3
Betty Dob. Coz [Cousin]	21½	0 – 10 – 9
Bess Dawson	26	0 – 13 – 0
Wilcock Mary	21½	0 – 10 – 9
Wetherhead	22	0 – 11 –
Morrison	20	0 – 10 – 0
Popleton wife	26½	0 – 13 – 3
Harrison Bett. Wife	17	0 – 8 – 6
Cawood lad	a day	0 – 0 – 2

(WYL100/EA/12/19 WYAS)

Clearly the women were paid on a daily basis at 3d per day, except for 'the lad', who only earned 2d. It would have been interesting to have known how old he was. We assume that married women were denoted by 'wife', although this may also refer to them as being specifically wives of other estate workers. 'Old' Hardy is a woman of advanced years and one woman is denoted as 'Widd.', being a widow. Others named are presumably single or younger women.

Garden labourers are also detailed, as here for the period 13 August to 8 September 1759. Interestingly, this record shows both male and female workers:

24 [days]	John Ward	1 – 4 – 0
21	Rich. Powell	1 – 1 – 0
24	Saml Roberts	1 – 4 – 0
24	Wm Atkinson	1 – 4 – 0
12	John Holland	12 – 0
24	Sarah Rawdon	9 – 7
20 ½	Ann Bland	8 – 6 ½
22 ½	Eliz. Prince	8 – 11 ½

To Richd. Powell for (–) eggs for the pheasants. Nine times at eight pence each time   6 - 0

The men earned a flat rate of 1s per day, whereas the women earned less than half of that at approximately 5¾d each day! Their work was probably no less arduous than the men's and it would be another forty years before Mary Wollstonecraft wrote her seminal feminist work, *A Vindication of the Rights of Woman*.

Labourers' wages, all male, for May 1759, were given as:

Joseph Ellis	6 days	0 – 5 – 0
Joseph Wainwright	6 days	0 – 5 – 0
Joseph Hardwick	6 days	0 – 5 – 0
Wm Millner	6 days	0 – 5 – 0
John Brown	6 days	0 – 2 – 0
Joseph Denison	6 days	0 – 2 – 0
Richd. Fenton	6 days	0 – 2 – 0

Perhaps labouring was not as skilled as garden labouring, for the above were earning only 10d per day for a six-day week. The last three named are presumably boys, as they are earning under half the men's wages. However, by August of the same year, there had been a wage rise for the labourers. Accounts show that they were now earning 1s per day, but the boys were still only earning the same. The list of names remained the same, with the addition of an Abraham Denison, who earned 2s for his six days' work. Clearly a boy, could he have been a younger brother of Joseph Denison?

Often servants were just recorded by the role or function they served on the estate, as in this 1758 list of male servants at Temple Newsam and their annual wages paid in pounds, shillings and pence:

Lord Irwin's gentleman	20- 0-0
4 Footmen	6-10-0 [each]
1 Butler	8- 0-0
1 Cook	12- 0-0
1 Husbandman [Stockman]	8- 0-0
1 Keeper [Gamekeeper]	10- 0-0
1 Coachman	12- 0-0
1 Postillion	5-10-0
1 Helper [?]	6-10-0
2 Grooms and a boy	12- 0-0 [in total?]
1 Gardner	10- 0-0
1 Caterer	[no sum recorded]
1 Pantry man	[no sum recorded]

The National Archives give a value of £1 in 1760 being equivalent to approximately £75 today, so from the figures above we can see the hierarchy of Lord Irwin's Gentleman being paid £20 (£1,500 today), to the lower ranking postillion earning just £5 10s (£412.50). Perhaps the cook and pantry man earned even less, as no figure is recorded.

Browsing through newspapers of the period can also give information on servants and estate workers. In this particular case, we learn it through a tragic incident:

On Tuesday, as John Bywater, aged seventeen, (nephew of Mr Thomas Bywater head farmer to her Grace the Marchioness of Hertford) was engaged with a cart and horse, in conveying ice from the fish pond in the grounds at Temple Newsam, to the ice-house, his foot slipped and the cart wheel went over his head, by which accident the unfortunate young man was so severely injured as to cause his death. This fatal event is a source of great grief to the family of the deceased, as well as of regret to his numerous friends, by whom he was greatly respected.

(*The Leeds Intelligencer*, 22 January 1829)

And again, later, in 1885:

An inquiry was held … on the body of James Nettleship, labourer, employed by Mrs Meynell-Ingram of Temple Newsam. Deceased was driving a steam cultivator when, on taking too short a turn at the headland, the machine turned over upon him, and he was dragged under it ten yards. He died almost immediately.

(*The Illustrated Police News*, 25 July 1885)

A good servant was valuable and sometimes they were cared for at their employer's expense. In the series WYL100/EA/12/19, the Temple Newsam collection, at the West Yorkshire Archives, there is an expense account for monies paid for in the nursing of Sarah Thrush, a servant girl, who had smallpox. Unfortunately, the document is not dated, but the term of address 'Goode' for a woman was becoming out of date by the mid-eighteenth century, and the style of script could indicate some point in the early eighteenth century:

The Expense of Sarah Thrush having the Small Pox

May 1;	gave Joan Forman for Sarah	0 – 8 – 0
	gave Mrs Ride for Sarah	0 – 10 – 0
May 15;	pd. Joan Forman for 3 weeks	
	attendance & board	1 – 19 – 0
	gave Goode Weller for Sarah	1 – 10 – 0
	gave Joan Forman for Sarah	0 – 15 – 0

gave Will. Edws. For carrying things
for 3 weeks to and from the Rest House   0 – 6 – 0
spent at carrying Sarah to the Rest House   0 – 2 – 6
pd. For ½ load of wood   0 – 8 – 0
pd. Goode Weller for 4 weeks board
and tendance in money twenty 2 shill;
and outset 30/ she owed   2 – 12 – 0

Sarah was obviously a well valued member of the household but it is not recorded if she survived or not.

Another important figure on the estate was that of the gamekeeper. His job was to manage the area of the estate and to ensure that there was enough game for shooting and fishing, and sometimes in earlier days, hunting. He would also be responsible for preventing poaching or apprehending poachers. Gamekeepers had long had the power to arrest poachers. This could be a difficult task if the estate was very large and usually a head 'keeper' had a small team working under him. It could also be a dangerous job. Game Laws favoured the aristocracy but an increasing population, particularly during the period of industrialisation, led to many of the poorer people taking game birds and animals from the estates of the gentry. If you were poor and hungry and needed to feed your family it seemed iniquitous to many that landowners should keep game purely for their own pleasure in hunting. The taking of game became a quite widespread, although potentially risky, affair. The 1723 Black Act made it illegal to enter onto a private estate armed and with a black face (or otherwise disguised) with the intention of taking game. If caught, it could mean a fine in the first instance, transportation for further offences, or even death. Just over 100 years later, in 1828, the Night Poaching Act was brought into power. In this, anyone taking or destroying game by night would be committed to fines and increasing lengths of imprisonment with hard labour, according to the number of offences committed. In the extreme case, usually after the third offence, the offender was liable to transportation. If these laws were not deterrent enough, gamekeepers set mantraps and spring guns around their estates to frighten off would-be poachers. Often the poachers were given fair warning of the installation of these preventative measures, with warnings being printed in newspapers, as here in *The Leeds Intelligencer* of 5 October 1826:

CAUTION – MEN TRAPS AND SPRING GUNS are set in all the Woods, Plantations, and Pleasure Grounds, belonging to the Marchioness of Hertford, Temple Newsam.

This presupposes that poachers are people who read newspapers, especially the 'small ads'. However, the setting of these quite violent instruments did not deter the poachers. *The Leeds Intelligencer* of 21 December 1826 gave a lengthy report of an 'Affray with Poachers'. Six poachers were apprehended and two managed to escape, but not without injury. One was so dangerously wounded in his right arm and back that he was not expected to survive many hours, and another was wounded in the arm. No gamekeepers were injured in the affray. Contrary to what might be thought, the poachers were not destitute or without work; they were reported as two glass-blowers, a pork butcher, a sawyer, and a cloth weaver. The statement given by Thomas Phillips, assistant gamekeeper, is worth recording in some detail, as it gives a first-hand account of the very real dangers facing keepers:

on Monday morning, the 17th December, he went into the park at Templenewsam [*sic*] ... between one and two o'clock, in consequence of hearing guns fired, and went in search of poachers with Thos. Shaw, Robt. Shaw, John Shaw, Jas. Pennington, Joseph Hebdin and Reuben Phillips. ... He and his party laid in wait for the poachers. ... But afterwards pursued them across the Park and met with them in Edw. Phillip's close, and went up to them, when they swore they would blow his brains out (he being the first of his party) if he did not stand back. He said, 'friends mind what you are going to do.' They still persisted in the same language and John Jackson [a poacher] then said he would blow his brains out if he did not stand further back, and put his gun up to his shoulder, pointed it, and swore and swore he would blow witness's brains out. ... Witness had a dog in [*sic*] a string, which he let go at them ... and immediately the whole of the poachers, eight in number, cried out, 'shoot the dog', and immediately a gun was fired at the dog by Jackson. One of the poachers, dressed in a dark coloured coat, then fired at his (Phillips') party, which was returned by the keepers, who followed them.

In defence, James Rider claimed that the keepers had set dogs on them and that only two shots were fired by the poachers, at the dogs. Four of the poachers were found guilty and sent to the Wakefield House of Correction to await trial with an application for bail being refused. James Rider was not on the guilty list, so possibly he was acquitted, and his severely wounded brother Richard is not mentioned at all, so did he die of his wounds? The two others who escaped were presumably still on the run.

Sometimes the odds were stacked against the keepers, as poachers took to hunting in gangs so large in number that the poachers could do little about it:

On Wednesday night, a large body of poachers, to the number of between sixty and seventy, assembled on the grounds of the Marchioness of Hertford, at Temple Newsam, ten of whom were armed with guns, the rest had sticks an bludgeons. Emboldened by their numbers, they approached the house, and shot pheasants close to the mansion. The keepers and watchers did not venture to oppose any resistance to so formidable a body, but sent an express early in the morning, to our Courthouse, for assistance. It was impossible to take the watchmen from their rounds, but, at six o'clock in the morning ... upwards of thirty were mustered, and dispatched to Temple Newsam, by different routes, but fortunately, they did not fall in with the poachers; if they had, it is probable that more than one life would have been lost. ... We believe that none of the party has yet been apprehended.

(*The Leeds Mercury*, 25 December 1827)

Outrageous attacks by such large bodies of poachers prompted advertisements being placed in local newspapers with offers of rewards for information, as here, complete with all the rogue capital letters:

POACHERS – TWENTY GUINEAS REWARD
Whereas, on the Night of Monday last, the fifteenth of December, a Large Body of Armed POACHERS were assembled with Fire Arms, in the Grounds and Park of the Marchioness of Hertford, at Temple Newsam, for the Purpose of DESTROYING GAME, in such Formidable numbers as to overpower the Keepers and Watchers, a REWARD of TWENTY GUINEAS is hereby offered to any Person who shall give such Information as may lead to the Conviction of any one or more of the Offenders.

(*The Leeds Intelligencer*, 25 December 1828)

This was a handsome reward, worth just over £1,000 today. We do not know if information was gathered from this offer, but poaching continued unabated and there was much debate in the press as to whether upholding the Game Laws, for the privilege of the few, was worth the risk to keepers.

We hope that these laws [Game Law] will be brought before Parliament Session after Session until some change has been made in them, which will do away with their manifold and serious evils … We believe that, if a strict and accurate account were kept of all the murders and executions which arise [out of violation of the Game Laws], it would be found that they cost little, if at all, less than fifty lives per annum. … There is, in fact, a complete guerrilla warfare raging in many parts of the country. … The law is therefore as ineffectual as it is injurious; it affords no protection to the game of the land-owners, while it ruins the morals of their tenantry.

(*The Leeds Mercury*, 21 February 1829)

In 1848, a Bill to repeal the Game Laws was put to vote in Parliament – and was narrowly defeated. The laws passed in the nineteenth century are still, in a moderated form, in use today. Poaching on the Temple Newsam estate continued into the twentieth century, and even during the First World War there were instances recorded in the press:

Joseph Swaine ... was yesterday committed for trial ... for offences connected with an alleged serious poaching affray on the estate of the Hon. E. Wood of Temple Newsam, Leeds on November 5th. The prisoner was charged with night poaching with arms, and with unlawfully wounding Robert Robinson and John Pullan, two gamekeepers.

(*The Leeds Mercury*, 25 November 1914)

In this instance, Joseph Swaine was committed for trial after a lengthy period in remand due to the injuries sustained by the gamekeepers.

Many large estates, Temple Newsam amongst them, leased land to tenant farmers. Although not strictly employed by the estate, they did contribute to its management. In this way the land was maintained and rents could be gathered to add to estate coffers. The terms and conditions of lease offered by the Marquis of Hertford to his tenants at Temple Newsam are quite strict. Rents had to be paid half yearly. The tenants had to pay all parochial and parliamentary taxes and tithes. The buildings had to be maintained in a good and tenantable repair. All produce, both for human and animal consumption, had to be consumed on the farm and not elsewhere. Similarly, all dung, compost and manure had to be used on the farm or land. A tenant could be removed from his farm, with a six months' notice. If he should overstay this period he could be liable to a penalty of £100 with an additional rent of £20 per acre held. The names of tenants are largely lost but sometimes their names are recorded in the manorial courts records, as for example these all recorded for 10 August 1722 (WYL 100/M/1-11 WYAS):

for the seizure of lands and property of Michael Gravely; Mich. Gravely of Halton or some other person lately made or caused to be made (bricks) and taken away without the Lord of the Manor's knowledge or consent contrary to the custom as appears by a Jury's verdict the 4th day of October last.

The seizure of lands and premises of William Broadbent of Halton for cutting or causing to be cut and taking away trees.

The seizure of lands and premises of Richard Reynolds of Halton Moor for failure to maintain repair.

And in 1754:

> The seizure of property of widow Bland in light of her husband being convicted and executed for felony.

But these were people who were required to be named because of their particular transgressions.

Occasionally we can learn much more about an individual, particularly if they were a trusted servant or of high enough status within the household. This is especially true of the stewards. A steward would have a wide-ranging role and his duties would include, amongst others, general estate management, the collection of rents, the holding of manorial and other courts, being responsible for leases, the oversight of pastures and mills, the oversight of farming operations, the selling of produce and stock and dealing with defaulting tenants and poachers. This was a responsible position within the estate and one that was legally arranged. On 1 September 1661, Sir Arthur Ingram III appointed one John Richardson, Scrivener, of Halifax to be steward of his manor of Halifax. The document does not detail his duties, apart from 'to keep the Courts for my Manor of Halifax'. A later appointment by the Marquis of Hertford (Francis Ingram Seymour-Conway) and his wife Isabella Ann Shepheard Ingram, in 1809, appointed John Pemberton Haywood as Steward of Temple Newsam. In this document there are a few more details of responsibility, particularly where the courts are concerned:

> Know all men by these presents that we Francis Ingram Marquis of Hertford and Isabella Anne Shepheard Ingram Marchioness of Hertford his wife Have constituted and appointed and by these presents to constitute and appoint John Pemberton Haywood of Wakefield in the County of York Esquire Steward of our ... Manor or Lordship of Temple Newsam ... giving and granting ... full power and authority to keep and hold all and every the Courts Leet, Courts Baron, Views of Frank , Courts Customary, and other courts ... within the said Manor ... and to ask demand and receive from longholders and leaseholders all rents and leased.
>
> [signed and sealed] Ingram Hertford
M. I.S. Hertford
(WYL160/213/84 WYAS, 13 November 1809)

The courts listed date back to medieval times, when a lord of a manor could exercise certain jurisdictional rights over his tenants. These were carried out through his court baron. This court had no power over criminal matters. However, a lord of the manor could be granted further powers by the Crown. One of these was the view of frankpledge. This was a system of engendering a shared responsibility among a group of households, usually ten in number. The leader of each group, often known as a tithing-man, would be responsible for bringing any wrongdoer from within the group to the court. If he failed to appear then the whole group would be fined or punished. The court leet was the jurisdiction over part of a county and could be held by the lord of the manor. The courts leet began to decline as the system of justices of the peace and magistrates' courts were developed but they continued in some places until their formal abolition in 1998. There are still some two dozen places in England and Wales that still retain a court leet but these have either limited or ceremonial powers.

One of the more noted and recorded stewards of Temple Newsam was John Matteson (Mattison). In fact, there were two John Mattesons, an uncle and nephew, who served Sir Arthur Ingram (senior and junior) and their estates. John Matteson senior had worked for two other masters before he came to be in service with Sir Arthur Ingram. Documents in the West Yorkshire Archives show that in 1603/4 he was servant to John Priestley and that by 1609 he was a servant to David Waterhouse (WYL100EA/18/8/5 and WYL100EA/18/8/16). At what point he entered into service with Ingram is not exactly known. Certainly he was with Waterhouse during 1610, as several letters to him at this time refer to him being in Okewell, near Birstall, which was the home of Waterhouse:

William Mooke at Birstall to John Mattison at Mr David Waterhouse's house at Okewell. Wanting an appointment to see him and complaining of his treatment, having come from Howley to see him.

(WYL100/OA/D/10, 16 August 1610)

By September the following year, it would appear that Matteson may have been in the process of moving to Ingram. A letter to him of 18 September:

Robert Danyell to John Mattison at Okewell about his horse ... to let him know how things are likely to be settled at Okewell and also whether Mr Ingram hath sealed your lease or no.

(WYL100/OA/D/19, 18 September 1611)

As well as his more formal duties in service, letters held by the West Yorkshire Archive Service, series WYL100/OA/D/, give us a fascinating insight into the more general life of the period:

Thomas Mattison to his brother John Mattison at Okewell. Hoping to effect the business which John had written about and expecting to see him within 14 days after Michaelmas. Brother Walter at Ampleforth had a son Walter christened last Sunday.

(WYL100/OA/D/11, 21 September 1610)

Robert Danyell to John Mattison at Okewell inquiring if his nagg be recovered and promising to send jerkin to James Lee.

(WYL100/OA/D/12, 3 November 1610)

George Pewtinger to John Mattison at Okewell. I have given the drawneworkes to Christian's sister ... so soon as they be done I will send them. I have sent by Clarkson Christian's bodyes and other things. Your stockins I remember but have not changed them ... Let Mistress Elizabeth know I have sent her measure to Mr Thorpe 5 or 6 weeks ago to buy her fardingale it being a thing whereof I am not acquainted.

(WYL100/OA/D/25, 1610)

By 1612, John Matteson senior was in service with Sir Arthur Ingram. He became a trusted employee and, in time, was responsible for Ingram's affairs in the north of England, particularly in respect of his estates at Temple Newsam, York and Sherriff Hutton. By the time that Ingram had purchased Temple Newsam and was beginning the rebuilding process, a process that would last many years, Matteson was negotiating and issuing contracts for the work to be done:

Francis Gumby of Temple Newsam joiner with Sir Arthur Ingram to make and set up where Sir Arthur shall appoint 400 yds of wanscott or selling at 12d a yard. Gunby to find all substances and utensils save only nails and deals. £5 already received and £5 at the finishing of each 100 yards.

(WYL100/EA/13/71/2, 18 February 1628)

For work to be done in the Gallery as in the Parlour made between Sir Arthur Ingram and Nicholas Booth, plasterer. To frett the gallery, architrave freeze [frieze] and cornice to be a yeard deep … to wainscot the gallery with fir deals.

(WYL100/EA/13/71/1, c.1628)

Between John Matteson (on behalf of Sir Arthur Ingram of York) and James Cooke and William Peas of Hawton brickmaker 'to make or cause to be made 150,000 bricks at Temple Newsam … the like measure in breadth length and thickness as the other bricks formerly made there or at Sheriff Hutton':

    For the sum of 3s 4d for every thousand;
    £3 15s 0d at the digging of the clay;
    £3 15s 0d at the turning and tempering of the clay;

The rest at several times … vix 1st April next, £3 10s. 0d, 1st May next £3 10s 0d and so … until the sum of £25 be paid;

Brickmakers to begin in March next or sooner if weather will permit;

Sir Arthur to provide at his own cost and charges at Temple Newsam, straw wood or coles found needful and necessary for the making and burning of the said 150,000 bricks;

Cooke and Peas to be jointly bound in £40.

Signed by mark.

Witnesses (by mark) Christopher Norton, William Drew, Luke Grenebere.

Memo. that Walter Armstrong of York brickmaker binds himself to observe and perform all articles which the above bound Cooke and Peas are bound to observe.

(WYL100EA/13/71/3, 22 March 1631/2)

The bricks used to rebuild Temple Newsam were obviously of a good quality for in 1636, Ingram contracted Richard Fisher of York, brickmaker, and Christopher Walker of Whitkirk (within the Manor of Temple Newsam) to provide:

200,000 bricks at the rate of 3s 4d the thousand, good, hard, well burned merchantable bricks of the size as they have lately made at Temple Newsam … 100,000 before 28 May next the other 100,000 before 28th Aug. next; to be paid £36 6s 8d; viz. £4 at the digging of the clay, £4 at the first turning and tempering of the clay, £4 at the second turning and 40s every 14 days until the sum of £36 6s 8d be paid.

(WYL100/EA/13/71/5, 20 October 1636)

John Matteson was clearly efficient at his job and rose in esteem over the years. As a result of the responsibilities placed upon him by Ingram he became more of a partner to Ingram rather than simply a servant. Both Mattesons, in their time, acted as Ingram's treasurer for his affairs in Yorkshire. They were responsible, in the name of Sir Arthur Ingram, for gathering rents, paying debts, negotiating loans, dealing with creditors, financing building works and buying land as instructed. It was a powerful position to hold and sometimes a thankless undertaking. Often significantly large amounts of money would need handling and occasionally Ingram would ask, or even expect, Matteson to pay bills from his own account. Presumably he was reimbursed at a later date. In connection with the financial problems Ingram had with his alum business, particularly in and around 1624, he even asked Matteson to stand him credit. A.F. Upton (1961) refers to the fact that Matteson forwarded in the region of £1,000 to the alum works. Much of this sum was raised through the collection of rents, the calling in of debts and raising loans where he could. But some of the money was put up by him. Ingram wrote to him at the time:

For your own money, I will take such a course as shall give you great content, and therefore I pray you pay all you can, for it stands me much upon.

(A.F. Upton, 1961)

Letters between Matteson and Ingram (held by the WYAS in series WYL100/C4) reveal just how much financial business Matteson undertook for his master. In April 1642, Matteson wrote to Ingram concerning the need to repay a bill:

is a letter & a bill of [-] within it for the repayment of thirty pounds to Mr John Sympson which I sent to you with £100 for my master by William Pell.

(22 April 1642)

In the June of that year, only a matter of months before his own death, Ingram wrote to Matteson:

John Mattison. I am to pay unto my Lord Aubigny of Yorke the sum of too [sic] hundred pounds. I pray when his Lordship shall bring or send this my letter unto you that presently upon the sight thereof you may pay unto my Lord or such as he shall appoint the said two hundred pounds and I pray you see this very carefully done for it doth much concern me and take hereunder a receipt so much paid.

(27 June 1642)

Was Ingram concerned that the correct amount should be paid or was he more concerned about the fact that he owed the money? In any case, the bill was paid and the letter was receipted signed 'Aubigny', dated July 1642. On 11 July, Ingram sent yet another letter to Matteson:

John Mattison. I pray you pay unto my noble lord the Lord Aubigny or such as he shall appoint the some of one hundred pounds. I pray you make good payment hereof upon sight of this my letter and take a receipt hereof written under his Lordships hand for so much as promised accordingly and this shall be your discharge.

(11 July 1642)

Again, this was paid and receipted as instructed. John Matteson proved a loyal servant and friend to his master. These were significant amounts of money; £100 of that time was equivalent to approximately £8,500 today. So, with the two payments mentioned above, Ingram was owed by Lord Aubigny an equivalent of in excess of £25,000. We have to assume that Matteson had access to ready cash in order for these payments to be made in full. What these payments were for is not exactly known but the Lord Aubigny mentioned was the 9th Seigneur d'Aubigny and was son of the 3rd Duke of Lennox, from whom Ingram had bought the Temple Newsam estate. Whatever the payments were for, Lord George d'Aubigny was killed at the Battle of Edgehill a few months later, in October 1642.

Matteson travelled widely in his duties. In a letter of August 1642 to Christopher Ellison, the servant of Thomas Ingram (Sir Arthur's son), he describes how he had been to Cleveland to enquire as to the Glebe of Seamore and the tithes of Middleton and Hilton. After the death of Sir Arthur Ingram senior, John Matteson the younger continued working for Sir Arthur Ingram junior.

Travelling at that time was becoming increasingly more difficult. As the constraints of the Civil War began to bite, so any unauthorised travellers were liable to arrest under military law. Hostilities were in full force by this time. In January 1643, Parliamentarian forces under Sir Thomas Fairfax had taken the Royalist garrison at Leeds. Fortunately, Temple Newsam was unaffected by this action, being a few miles from the city, although the Parliament supporting Sir Arthur Ingram junior must have been pleased at this. Later, in March 1643, another battle took place at Seacroft Moor, to the north-east of Leeds. Fairfax's troops had attacked and dismantled the Royalist holding at Tadcaster and were returning to Leeds. They were attacked by a Royalist force and were defeated, the remnants of the Parliamentarian troops fighting their way through to Leeds. This is probably the nearest military action got to Temple Newsam, as Seacroft falls within the northern limits of the manor, and perhaps Ingram felt alarmed at this.

York was a Royalist stronghold and in order to travel safely around the area, Matteson required letters of permission, as here on the authority of the Marquis of Newcastle, Commander in Chief of the King's northern forces:

Permit Mr John Mattison and his servant Richard Stones of this Citty quietly to passe unto Kilbington B[-] Whitwell in the Wynd and Hutton Rudby in ye County of York and to passe to this Citty … without trouble or molistation. Given under my hand this fifth of April 1644.

(WYL100/PO/2/A/I/32, 5 April 1644)

This letter of permit was issued only a few days before Parliamentarian forces laid siege to the city. During June, York was heavily bombarded, besiegers took horses and cattle and food was rationed. Where was Matteson during all of this? It is not known whether he was in York or at Temple Newsam or one of the other Ingram Yorkshire properties. The Royalist forces were finally defeated at Marston Moor, a few miles from York, on 2 July 1644, but the siege continued until 16 July, when York came under the rule of Parliamentarian forces, commanded by Sir Thomas Fairfax. A new regime was established in York but still under martial law. It would seem that Sir Thomas Fairfax established his headquarters at the York home of the Ingrams, as indicated by the contents of this note signed by Thomas Fairfax:

The C[ommander] to forbear the demanding of any [-] of Mr Jn Maddison for any rooms belonging to the house wherein my quarters are.

[signed] T. Fairfax
(WYL100/PO/2/A/I/39, April 1645)

By May 1645, Fairfax had been replaced by Sidenham Poyntz, a seasoned soldier in the Thirty Years' War. He was made Commander in Chief of the northern Association Army. Matteson continued to travel around the county on Ingram business and now had letters of permission signed by Poyntz:

> Permitt and suffer ye body of Mr John Mattison with his servant and horses quietly to pass from place to place within ye Countie of York about his lawful occasions without interupon [interruption] Provided they go not into any of ye King's Garrisons or Quarters nor [–] anything p[–]ial to ye Stables & Garrison at York.
>
> Ye xxviith day of July 1645
To all officers & soldiers
In ye service of the State
>
> [signed] Sednham Poynts
(WYL100/PO/2/A/I/37, 24 July 1645)

It is unusual to find so much recorded about a particular servant but, as we have seen, both John Mattesons were far more than just employees; they were loyal and trusted friends and highly valuable to both Sir Arthur Ingrams. Servants of all description and function oiled the machinery that kept the great estates like Temple Newsam fully operational. Without them, the estate would have been nothing. It is often too easy to overlook the presence of this hidden army as we stroll around the estate today.

Chapter 8

A Benevolent House

Mrs Meynell-Ingram, the chatelaine of Temple Newsam

When Isabella Ingram Seymour-Conway, the Marchioness of Hertford, died in 1807, the estates at Temple Newsam and at Hoar Cross in Staffordshire passed firstly to her sister Frances, the second daughter of the 9th Viscount Irwin. Temple Newsam remained in her control until she died in 1841, when the estates should have passed to her sister Elizabeth, who had married Hugo Meynell. Unfortunately, Elizabeth had predeceased her sisters; as there were no children from the marriage, the estates passed to her nephew, Hugo Charles Meynell. Although Isabella had directed in her will that Ingram should be attached to the name Meynell, it was Hugo Charles that eventually took the name Meynell-Ingram, and so perpetuated Temple Newsam's long association with that illustrious name.

Whilst Isabella had brought about some further developments to Temple Newsam House during her tenure, little was done during the time of Frances and Hugo Charles. In fact, the only significant event was the visit of the Prince of Wales in May 1868, which was hosted by his eldest son, Hugo Francis Meynell-Ingram, his father being too infirm to attend. The Prince was visiting Leeds to inaugurate the Fine Art Exhibition in the New Infirmary. Newly opened, the building comprised ten spacious wards with connecting staircases and corridors that provided ample display space for the exhibition of national treasures. The Prince arrived by train at the tiny village of Woodlesford and was met by an enthusiastic crowd that cheered him all the way to nearby Temple Newsam House:

> The reception of the Prince of Wales at Woodlesford station, on Monday afternoon, was sufficiently enthusiastic to give him a foretaste of the warmth of a Yorkshire welcome. ... By trains and by vehicles,

on foot and on horseback, people poured into Woodlesford in the most surprising manner. ... The crowds of vehicles drawn up by the sides of the road was very large, and the rocky slopes by the side of the road was thronged by men, women, and children, patiently awaiting the appearance of the Prince. ... Once clear of the denser portion of the spectators, the royal cortege proceeded at a rapid pace down the road toward Temple Newsam. ... Up to the entrance to the estate the road ... presented the appearance of the road to Epsom on a Derby day. ... At the entrance to Temple Newsam [on Bullerthorpe Lane], before the gateway was reached, the procession passed beneath a remarkably beautiful triumphal arch, composed of spruce fir, whose leaves were woven together.

(*The Yorkshire Post and Leeds Intelligencer Supplement*, 23 May 1868)

The jubilation at the Prince's visit was great and further celebratory triumphal arches had been erected along the avenue to the house and at the northern Whitkirk gate entrance. When the Prince left the house for Leeds the next morning he passed through further arches erected in the villages of Whitkirk and Halton to mark his passage to the city. On the Monday evening, a large concert, conducted by Mr Charles Hallé, founder of the Hallé Orchestra, was held in the house and many dukes and duchesses and lords and ladies were invited. The Prince's stay at Temple Newsam was just overnight but it shows the high esteem in which the estate was held.

Within a year of the Prince's visit, Hugo Charles had died at the age of eighty-five at his estate in Staffordshire; his wife, Georgiana (Piqou), had predeceased him by only a few months. He had been both a high sheriff of Yorkshire and of Staffordshire, but not such a prominent figure as some of his forebears may have been. He was well respected, as shown here in an obituary in *The Yorkshire Post and Leeds Intelligencer* of 1 March 1869:

The deceased did not take a prominent part in politics, but confined himself mostly to the conscientious discharge of those duties which his position as a country gentleman, a magistrate, and a landlord entailed upon him. In the latter capacity his tenantry found in him one anxious at all times to forward their interests; and his sociable, kindly disposition obtained for him the respect and esteem of those with whom he was on terms of intimacy, and indeed of all classes.

Hugo Francis inherited his father's estates, to the value of £160,000. Born in 1822, Hugo Francis made a name for himself as a Conservative Member of Parliament for West Staffordshire in 1868. He was also a Justice of the Peace for both Staffordshire and Derbyshire, and a captain in the Queen's Own Royal Staffordshire Yeomanry. In 1863, he married the Honourable Lady Emily Charlotte Wood, daughter of Sir Charles Wood, the 1st Viscount Halifax. The Meynell and the Wood families were on opposing political sides. Sir Charles Wood was a Whig politician and from 1846 to 1852, was Chancellor of the Exchequer. The Meynells were Conservative, so there is little surprise that the marriage between Hugo Francis and Emily was frowned upon. There was an eighteen-year age gap between them, but they were truly in love and married in 1864. Letters held in the Halifax collection (Borthwick catalogue) attest to their love, and when Hugo Francis inherited the estate they began to spend more time at Temple Newsam. Sadly, Emily had had an earlier riding accident that left her unable to have children. To compound this tragedy, Hugo Francis died after a short illness in 1871, only two years after inheriting Temple Newsam. He left an estate worth £180,000 (somewhere in the region of £9 million today) to his wife Emily but declared in his will that the house at Hoar Cross should be made over to his two sisters, Elizabeth and Georgiana, while they were unmarried. Emily now found herself widowed and childless at thirty-one years old, but very wealthy. In fact, she was listed as one of the top three wealthiest dowagers in the country.

After the death of her husband, Emily began to spend more and more time at Temple Newsam. It became her preferred residence, although she occasionally visited her other estate at Hoar Cross and spent time in London. She also liked overseas travel. She had had an interest in yachting for some years and owned her own private yacht, the *Ariadne*. Newspaper reports of the late nineteenth century often refer to her, and her invited parties, either travelling to meet the yacht in Algiers or her being in Rome, where her yacht was waiting for her at Naples. Even late in her life, in 1903, she was still travelling, and *The Leeds Mercury* notified its readers that she would be sailing on the yacht *Gitana* for several weeks. Her personal photograph albums, held now at Temple Newsam, record many of these foreign visits. The albums also show that she was quite well connected with notable members of society. Included in one album are several photographs of the young Prince of Wales, Albert Edward; later to become King Edward VII. But, for all her wealth and high-ranking connections, she did not forget the people around her. She was a philanthropist and many were the residents who benefitted from her, particularly those within her manors. She would open up her estate and house at Temple Newsam to entertain a variety of different groups. In June 1881, as recorded in *The Leeds Mercury* of 8 June, she made the park available for a three-day bazaar to raise funds for the completion of St Hilda's church. A large marquee was erected to the west of the house and many stalls were set up inside. Lady Meynell-Ingram took control of one stall and other notable ladies – the Countess of Zetland, Lady Mary Wood and the Hon. Mrs J. Dundas amongst others – all turned their hands to selling the variety of wares on offer. Other tents provided a range of amusements, including the Travelling Troubadours, Punch and Judy shows, telephones, and a strange and wonderful instrument called the dianthroposcope (an ingenious optical instrument whereby people could see through one another). For a small sum visitors could enter the house and marvel at the contents, all profits going to swell the funds. Lady Meynell-Ingram's philanthropic interests were wide and varied. Later in the same month, she hosted the Church of England Working Men's Society annual excursion. It was intended that tea should be served in the park, to be followed by evensong in the mansion chapel, but heavy rain prevented this and the group made a brief visit to the park before adjourning to nearby Whitkirk. Amongst other groups that she invited at various times were the Leeds and District Branch of the National Union of Elementary Teachers, and members of the Church of England Temperance Society, who held a large temperance festival in the grounds in 1885. *The Leeds Mercury* of 27 July gives a quite bucolic description of the event:

> A festival promoted by the Church of England Temperance Society was held on Saturday, in the grounds belonging to Mrs Meynell-Ingram, at Templenewsam, near Leeds. The lovely weather that prevailed tempted

many thousands of adults, as well as children, to take advantage of the opportunity this offered of visiting a place possessing so many attractions. The park presented an animated scene, and the gathering had the appearance of a gigantic picnic. The old folks, thankful for the protection afforded by the trees, lounged under their branches, listening to the music discoursed by the bands; while the young, for whose enjoyment special provision had been made, took part in various sports, including singing contests, skipping contests, and foot races … an enjoyable day in the country was brought to a conclusion by a display of fireworks.

Emily Meynell-Ingram was a generous benefactor to many. She supplied funding for the completion of two reredos in York Minster in 1884. When, in 1886, there was a serious underground explosion at the Altofts Colliery, near Wakefield, she immediately sent a telegram to offer any help that she could. Subsequently, she donated £200 to the relief fund. Later in her life, in 1903, she donated £800 towards the cost of building an institute for nearby Halton. This was to provide recreation, reading and bathrooms, with an additional hall and retiring room, for the use of the community. In the same year, the church of St Edward, in Holbeck, was endowed by Mrs Meynell-Ingram. She had also been responsible for the building of a new school and a vicarage. The total cost of this project was in excess of £30,000. Later, in 1899, when war broke out in the Transvaal against the Boers, she immediately donated £1,000 to provide transport for the Yorkshire Volunteers.

Although she had no children of her own, she was particularly interested in the needs of the children of Leeds. In 1894, she sold to the Hunslet Board of Guardians 4 acres of her land, at the village of Rothwell Haigh, in order that they should build a home for workhouse children. She was especially keen that children should receive religious instruction in school and spoke out strongly against Board schools, which, in her opinion, could not provide this. She was not afraid of controversy and actively spoke out against this lack of provision:

She made a vigorous speech … in which she said she felt it to be her paramount duty to keep out of the village the School Board education which a Government calling itself Liberal, but in reality hostile to religion, was forcing upon the country. ... Religious instruction could not be imparted by any teacher, however earnest and painstaking, who was not himself impressed with the force of religious truth.

(*The York Herald*, 11 June 1894)

This prompted a strong and immediate response from at least one teacher:

Mrs Ingram ... has apparently lost sight of the fact that there are thousands of teachers employed in Board Schools in England and Wales who were formerly in the service of the managers of Church of England schools. These teachers give religious instruction combined with moral training to Board School scholars of almost equal amount to that imparted to their former pupils in Church of England schools.

(*The York Herald*, 13 June 1894)

Her Catholic faith was very important to her. She was created a Dame of Grace of the Order of the Hospital of St John of Jerusalem. This is a royal order of chivalry and has a mission to 'prevent and relieve sickness and injury, and to act to enhance the health and well-being of people'. She would later be elevated to the rank of Dame of Justice within the Order by royal decree in 1902. With a philosophy based upon Christian values, she felt it vital that children should receive some form of religious education. She was especially supportive of the Sunday schools movement. In Queen Victoria's Jubilee year of 1887, Mrs Meynell-Ingram made an offer by letter to all superintendents of Sunday schools in the East Ward of Leeds:

I believe arrangements are being made by the school managers in Leeds to give their children a special treat in honour of the Queen's Jubilee. Should the Sunday school authorities of the East Ward not have fixed on any scheme at present, would you communicate to them from me how much pleasure it would give me to entertain the school children and their teachers at tea in the park at Templenewsam on a day shortly to be fixed.

(*The Leeds Mercury*, 8 June 1887)

Within a month, all the arrangements had been made, and on a Saturday afternoon in early July, the event took place:

> To a large class of the children of Leeds the name of the Hon. Mrs Meynell-Ingram is associated with some of the happiest experiences in their young lives. On Saturday afternoon, this lady added another to the list of benefactions which have gained her recognition as the 'children's friend'. Besides throwing open the beautiful grounds of Templenewsam to more than 5,000 boys and girls ... Mrs Meynell-Ingram treated each member of the small army with a substantial tea, and also provided various forms of outdoor recreation for her guests. ... The only qualification required by the children was that each recipient of the treat should be in attendance at some Sunday school. ... Before entering the grounds they formed into processional order, and, headed by the Leeds Artillery Band, marched past Mrs Meynell-Ingram, who was seated in a carriage at the Keeper's Gate. ... Although in delicate health, Mrs Meynell-Ingram spent nearly the whole afternoon and evening among her visitors.
>
> (*The Leeds Mercury*, 4 July 1887)

Ill health was a constant problem through the latter years of her life. She suffered from repeated bouts of influenza and several times visited a Professor Pagenstecker, in Wiesbaden, for treatment. Wiesbaden, in central Germany, was famous throughout Europe for its hot springs and medical treatments, and the rich and the famous frequently visited because of this. Although of a resilient character, she did suffer occasional accidents and shocks, such as an incident on Boar Lane, in Leeds, in early October 1894, when a handcart was hit by a bus and then thrown against the carriage of Mrs Meynell-Ingram. Although not physically injured, she was much disturbed.

The year 1894 saw the glittering highlight of her time at Temple Newsam. It was arranged for the Duke and Duchess of York, later to become King George V and Queen Mary, to visit Leeds in order to inaugurate both the new hall of the Yorkshire College and the new medical school. Mrs Meynell-Ingram would host the royal guests at Temple Newsam. On Thursday, 4 October, the royal party arrived by train at nearby Garforth railway station from Scotland, where they had previously been at Balmoral Castle. A large crowd of people were at the station and its surrounds to welcome the Duke and Duchess and their entourage. On the way to Temple Newsam, some 4 miles distant, the ways were lined with:

> bunting, here, there, and everywhere; at almost every turn the motto 'Welcome' greeted the eye, flags were hoisted in many likely and unlikely places, whilst the principle street of the village [Garforth] was resplendent with Venetian masts, streamers, trophies of flags, and heraldic shields.
>
> (*The Leeds Mercury*, 5 October 1894)

Admission to Temple Newsam park was by invitation only, and it is estimated that about 2,000 people, including most of Mrs Meynell-Ingram's tenantry, were waiting there to greet the visitors. That evening, a dinner was given in honour of the royal guests, to which Mrs Meynell-Ingram had invited a number of distinguished ladies and gentlemen. The Long Gallery was set for a table of forty-five and the above publication gave a very detailed description of the event. As you stand in the gallery today, it is not too hard to imagine the scene:

> A magnificent picture the room presented – its darkly polished oak floor, covered with strips of crimson carpet, and costly Oriental rugs, into which the foot sank luxuriously. The snowy white cloth threw into bolder relief the magnificent candelabras and epergnes [an ornamental table centrepiece], the gold and silver plate sent back the shaft of brilliant light that fell from above, while costly hot-house flowers lent their beauty and fragrance to the scene. Chairs, beautifully upholstered in all the colours of the rainbow, added to the splendour, and to this picture the walls hung with rarest treasures of the rarest art, formed a glorious setting. Two of Sir Joshua Reynolds' beauties smiled gaily on the scene; here a cavalier of Minevelt seemed about to step out of the restraining frame … masterpieces by Rembrandt, Vandyck, Holbein, Guido, Vandervelde, Titian, Bergognone, and Albert Dürer found

resting places here and there, and from a point of vantage the charming counterfeit of the hostess looked a kindly approval.

Mrs Meynell-Ingram's organisation as a hostess was well praised, but the same could not be said of the Leeds City Corporation. The day was marred by a series of blunders that caused much embarrassment to the city elders. On the morning of the royal visit to the city, the carriages that were to convey the Duke and Duchess and their party from Temple Newsam to the Town Hall failed to arrive, due to a series of misdirected orders. It was only Mrs Meynell-Ingram's quick thinking that saved the day, as she recorded in her diary for that day:

> The Duke & Duchess went into Leeds early, and had to be sent in with my horses and carriages as the Corporation ones failed. Landau with Touchstone and Shamrock, barouche with Templar and Primrose, sociable with Talisman ... and Duchess, Victoria with the chestnuts, the wagonette open with Harry and Dick and Charlie's carriage and horses conveyed the whole party with an escort of seventeen under Prince Adolphus of Teck.
>
> (Temple Newsam collection)

But this was only the first of several errors that could have spoiled the entire event. Embarrassment was caused when barriers, set up to block off certain streets to vehicles, were erected too early and the Corporation party were delayed in getting to the city boundary to meet their visitors. Fortunately, this was a minor incident because the royal party were delayed in leaving Temple Newsam! The procession into the city was directed to have been at a trot, and, had all carriage drivers followed this order, it should have arrived in the city as one unit. However, the procession became broken up and arrived in dribs and drabs. Further confusion was caused later when the Mayor's carriage was removed twice from its standing point outside the Town Hall and each time he had to reorder it back into position. When the royal party left the Town Hall it was found that the royal carriage had no footman. Unable to find one at short notice, the Mayor had to direct his mace bearer to act in that capacity. After delivering the guests to the various venues, it was discovered that the carriages were not arranged in the correct order to pick them up and, on two occasions, they had to be hastily rearranged. As a result of this catalogue of errors an inquiry was subsequently held.

By far the more serious event of the day was the perceived 'attack' on the royal carriage, although the Corporation could not have foreseen this. *The Leeds Mercury* of 8 October gives a detailed account of the incident:

> John Henry Thackrah rushed at the Royal carriage as it was passing along Park-row. … He seized the handle of the door of the Royal carriage, opened the door, and was in the act of springing in when Prince Adolphus of Teck [the younger brother of the Duchess], who was in command of the Lancers' escort, and who was riding immediately behind the right rear wheel (on the same side) rode at him. This prevented his entering the carriage, and His Serene Highness made a cut at the man with his sword, but missed him. … Thackrah still clung to the carriage door, and Sergeant Major Manning, who was riding on the other side, next made a cut at him, striking across the carriage in front of Their Royal Highnesses. He struck the man with the flat of his sword on the forearm, but still he retained his hold of the door, and the carriage went on with Thackrah hanging on to it. Then it was that Surgeon Captain De Burgh Birch [commander of the guard of honour at the side of the road] … ran forward and getting his right arm round Thackrah's neck, attempted to drag him off. At the same time, Private Hutchinson, a member of the company, hurried up and likewise laid hold of the man. The carriage door, coming open with a jerk, all three men went down together, Thackrah narrowly missing the wheel. … He was dragged aside and taken to the police station at the Town Hall. … His Royal Highness seemed little, if at all, discomposed by the sensational incident.

Thackrah was found to be unstable and charged with 'wandering abroad whilst apparently of unsound mine'. It was found that he posed no deliberate physical threat to either the Duke or Duchess; in fact, he claimed he had only wanted to shake the Duke's hand. It was recommended that he be sent to a public asylum, where he could receive the appropriate medical treatment.

The incident certainly did not distract from the 'At Home' given by Mrs Meynell-Ingram on Friday evening at Temple Newsam. The evening took place again in the Long Gallery but was not quite as formal as the previous dinner. As entertainment, two drawing room plays were presented before Their Royal Highnesses, and music was provided by the band of the Royal Artillery from London. The royal party left Temple Newsam the following morning, after official photographs had been taken and profuse thanks given to a generous hostess. I am sure that both the Duke and Duchess remembered their time in Leeds, for all sorts of different reasons.

During her time at Temple Newsam, Mrs Meynell-Ingram made many changes. Two of the most important were the introduction of electricity into parts of the building and the installation of oil-fired central heating. Some of the original radiators are still in place today, although now fuelled by gas. Both of these utilities were installed for the benefit of the royal visit. She also made some internal constructional changes to the building. The magnificent oak staircase, which is often mistaken as being original Jacobean, was actually created by Mrs Meynell-Ingram. Its intricate carvings are worth a detailed examination. The Jacobean style Entrance Hall and the panelled Darnley Room are also both later creations of hers, to create a romantic ambience.

Mrs Meynell-Ingram was one of the last great Victorian ladies, but times were changing. A new world was about to begin. She was the epitome of a Victorian dowager country lady; she loved horses, livestock, her estate and her tenants. Many were the agricultural fairs that she won prizes at for her livestock and her gardeners regularly won prizes at horticultural shows. In return for her benefaction, her tenants held her in high esteem. Photographs show her being drawn around the estate in a donkey cart, and she loved her horses. Her life had witnessed many new technologies, some of which she had openly embraced. Others, such as the motor car, she was reluctant to do so. Up until the turn of the century, there were no cars on her estate at Temple Newsam. She was not against progress but she did have to contend with the advent of the railways, the new roads, and the planned Leeds Corporation Sewage project. All of these would gradually encroach upon her estate and she must have felt that her way of life was being jeopardised. Even the proposed expansion of the city boundaries, to incorporate the villages of Halton, Whitkirk and neighbouring Crossgates, presented a threat. Today, the city boundary has expanded far beyond Temple Newsam to include many of the villages within her former manors.

By the early twentieth century, Mrs Meynell-Ingram was in decline. In November 1904, such was her illness that it was thought necessary to summon members of the family to her bedside at Temple Newsam. However, with characteristic dogged determination, she rallied and made a slight recovery. Unfortunately, her brother, Viscount Halifax, was not able to be present at his sister's side as he was on active military service in South Africa. Newspapers gave almost daily bulletins as to her condition but, by the middle of December, her condition was described as being critical and that she was sinking fast. She died, at the age of sixty-four, on the evening of Wednesday, 22 December from 'cardiac failure and exhaustion' (*Lichfield Mercury*) at her home at Temple Newsam. Her death was reported widely across the country but *The Yorkshire Post and Leeds Intelligencer* of 22 December summed up her life in a lengthy but glowing obituary, a sign of just how much she had contributed to society:

> We deeply regret to announce the death of the Hon. Mrs Meynell-Ingram. ... Comparatively few Leeds people knew Mrs Meynell-Ingram by sight. Only on rare occasions did she come prominently before the public. ... Her social influence, however, was often directed to benefit the city or some phase of life within it ... she took care not to lose touch with the varied interests lying around that historic mansion [Temple Newsam], and especially with Church matters in Whitkirk and Holbeck ... she dispensed no small part of it [her fortune] in the name of religion and charity. The full extent of the service that she rendered to others in this way will probably never be publicly known. Those who sought her bounty will recall how keenly alert she was to every detail. ... And once satisfied the desserts were ample she did not stint her aid ... she proved herself an admirable type of business woman, shrewd, capable, alive to all requirements, thoughtful of her tenantry, benevolent to the distressed, indulgent to those who differed from her, and ever mindful of her obligations as a Church-woman and a patron of church livings. ... In this and other respects she had all the characteristics of a Lady Bountiful.

Her body, enclosed in a shell and lead casket, was placed within a wedge-shaped polished oak coffin and transported to Hoar Cross for the funeral. She was interred in the family vault alongside the remains of her husband. Hundreds of people attended and special trains were laid on from Leeds to Burton-on-Trent, the nearest large town to Hoar Cross, so that the tenantry of Temple Newsam could attend.

And so ended the life of the last great Victorian chatelaine of Temple Newsam. The estate would now move on into a new and troubled world.

Chapter 9

A Haunted House

Ghostly tales from Temple Newsam

I t was early on a Sunday morning and Julie Holroyd, one of the visitor assistants at Temple Newsam House, was on cleaning duty before the house opened to the public. She was by herself and was vacuuming a carpet in one of the lower corridors, near the kitchens. This was a task she had regularly done and she was lost in her own thoughts. A movement caught her eye and she looked up. There, standing at the end of the corridor, was a young woman. She was dressed, as Julie described to me, in 'a pencil slim skirt and blouse and her hair was swept back with curls at each side. She looked as if she was dressed in the 1940s or 1950s. She looked at me and then turned into one of the rooms at the end of the corridor.' Knowing that there should have been nobody in the house at this time, Julie was momentarily taken by surprise, so she stopped her work and set off to see who this mysterious person was. The room at the end of the corridor was empty! Puzzled, Julie then looked around the area but could find no trace of the mysterious intruder.

This was only one of many strange occurrences over the years in Temple Newsam House. One of Julie's colleagues, Adrian Thompson, also recounts several events that he cannot explain. He was sitting with a colleague in an alcove of the west wing of the house, shortly before opening hour, when they both heard a tremendous crashing of glass from the north side of the house. Their first thoughts were that either a window had been smashed or something large had fallen from a wall, a rare but not unknown thing to happen. Looking across at the north wing there were no immediate signs of any window breakages so they ran around to that wing. All pictures in the Picture Gallery were in place and nothing had fallen, as far as they could see. They then ran up to the Bullion Room, which has a lot of glass display cabinets, but all was intact. They used their radios to contact staff in other areas of the house to see if anything had happened but the answer was no; everything was secure and there was nothing that could have caused such a noise. Yet both Adrian and his colleague had heard the noise that caused the alarm – another unexplained event.

Other strange happenings have also been simultaneously experienced by staff. Adrian and two colleagues were sitting in their staff room having their lunch. A movement caught his eye and he turned his head just in time to see a plastic food container rise off a cupboard in the corner and fly straight across the room and hit his male colleague on the back of the head. At the same moment, Jill, the other member of staff, turned to Adrian and asked, 'Did you see that or am I imagining it?' Both had witnessed the flying container but had no explanation as to how it could have happened. Melvyn, the third staff member, certainly felt the effects as he was hit on the back of the head. Although he accused the others of some practical joke at his expense, they steadfastly maintained what they saw.

Julie described another shared experience. Again, staff were in their staff room, which was below the Picture Gallery in the north wing, taking a break before opening the house to the public. All staff were there and nobody else was in the house – or nobody should have been! At that time a length of carpet ran down the whole length of the centre of the Gallery. Footsteps were heard above them, striding across the wooden floor and then pausing for a moment as they crossed the carpet, to continue a few seconds later. Knowing the house to be empty, the staff ran upstairs but there was no sign of anyone at all. The Picture Gallery was also the site of another incident experienced by Adrian. One of his duties before the house opens to the public is to ensure that everything is tidy. Around the Gallery there are several small lecterns, on which lie ring binders containing several, quite stiff to move, laminated pages of information. Adrian went round and made sure that all binders were neatly placed and open at the first page. A little while later, he returned to the Gallery for a final check, to find that all of the ring binders had been opened to different pages. His immediate thought was that some form of gust of wind had flipped them over but, as he explained, there were no open windows. It would have been impossible for a through draught to move the pages in this way because the lecterns were on both sides of the gallery and therefore could not all have been opened in the same way. Also, the pages are quite heavy and sometimes difficult for even visitors to move. Again, no rational explanation could be given.

Temple Newsam House has the accolade of being the most haunted house in Yorkshire. Whether the above incidents are manifestations of the alleged hauntings, who can say? However, Temple Newsam has hosted several 'paranormal nights' over the years. Adrian was present at one of them, as he describes here:

It was about five years ago now, we had a paranormal night on, I believe it was, a Sunday. It was one of the first ones we ever did. The last place we came to was the Bullion Rooms. There was a group of about ten of us up there, including myself, and I positioned myself midway between both the main Bullion Room and the small Bullion Room so I could see the whole scope of who was standing where, because obviously my job was to see that everything was safe. The lady who was leading the investigation started to ask some questions like, 'are you a male, are you female etc.' To get a response we wanted them to make a sound, and every time she asked a question, on cue, we would get a bang on the glass. Obviously, as I say, I had a view of all the guests who were there that night and none of them were near the end of the cabinets. I was there to make sure that none of them played a trick. None of them moved at all and every time the lady asked a question we got a response straight away, either one knock or two. That happened on six occasions. It was either [laughs] very good timing or there was something there. I could see everyone in my eye line and nobody was near the cabinets. It was certainly unexplained.

Strange sounds and objects being moved are all part of the catalogue of unexplained 'happenings' in the house. Physical 'appearances', as Julie witnessed, occur less often. Les, now retired from the house, was on duty at the main reception desk in the Great Hall. A man walked in through the entrance and turned immediately left into the Gentlemen's Passage leading to Mr Wood's Library. Having to pay an admission fee, Les immediately ran after him calling, 'Excuse me, excuse me, sir, have you got your ticket?'

He went down the corridor to Mr Wood's Library, went round and came back through the Chinese Room – but there was nobody there at all. As Les recounted, it was only a matter of seconds before he went after the man and it would have been impossible for him to lose sight of him.

All of the above are relatively recent happenings but historically there have been many more sightings and occurrences that defy rational explanation. In the Darnley Room it has been recorded in the past that a small boy appears from a cupboard and wanders around the room, looking a little lost before returning to the cupboard. Who this boy is supposed to be, or why he should appear to reside in a cupboard, nobody seems to know. The sound of children laughing and playing has often been heard at various points around the house. Another strange apparition claimed to have been seen in the same room is that of a fully regaled Knight Templar. There is logic to this sighting, as Temple Newsam did have a Templar preceptory on the estate some 900 years ago, although it was not on the site of the current house. There may have been a building on the site and perhaps it did have a connection with the Templars, but why the knight should choose to appear in the Darnley Room is somewhat baffling. Another ghostly figure occasionally seen scuttling around the grounds at night is that of a hooded monk. Sometimes he has been seen in the Long Gallery, moving towards the Chapel before he disappears. On other occasions he seems to set off across the lawns towards the south of the estate, heading towards the river Aire. Although seen, he never leaves any footprints. This was the area in which the Templars had their preceptory, so perhaps there is a connection. Certainly people have been disturbed enough by these visions. On a visit to Temple Newsam House in 1953, a man on business there excused himself to the director of the house, Mr Musgrave, from going upstairs. It would appear that:

Some years previously the man and his wife had been alone in the Long Gallery, at the far end near the Chapel. From a door in the side of the room the man saw a monkish figure in a brown habit emerge. It walked into the Chapel and crossed it in the direction of the organ, suddenly vanishing. His wife, too, saw the figure. She said, 'What's happened? Did you see that?' 'And,' said the man to Mr Musgrave, 'if you paid me money I wouldn't go into that Long Gallery again, nor would my wife. It was the most malevolent looking creature I ever saw.'

(*The Yorkshire Evening Post*, 10 October 1953)

A Mr Vickers, one of the foremen of Temple Newsam in the 1950s, also claimed to have seen some form of apparition in the same Long Gallery while he was alone doing his evening rounds. Very occasionally it has been recorded that an ethereal carriage and horses is seen driving towards the house along the drive from the eastern entrance to the estate on Bullerthorpe Lane. Other sightings relate specifically to historical figures connected with the house. You may recall from an earlier chapter that Lord Thomas Darcy was beheaded by King Henry VIII for his part in the rebellious Pilgrimage of Grace. It has been reported that his headless body has been seen riding through the grounds on moonlit nights.

Sightings of the 'White Lady' have been few and far between. K. Goor (2006) cites only two instances in which two serving maids, 160 years apart, witnessed the same apparition and gave the same matching description. The White Lady is reputed to be Lady Jane Grey, who, some claim, fell so in love with Lord Darnley and was so grief-stricken when he married Mary Queen of Scots, that she hanged herself. There are some fundamental flaws to this story that raise questions over the validity of the apparition. Lady Jane Grey, who later became Lady Jane Dudley on marriage in 1553, was born in 1536 and would have been nine years old when Darnley was born in 1545. Lady Dudley became England's 'Nine-Day Queen' when she acceded to the throne in 1553, after the death of her cousin Edward VI. On his deathbed he nominated Jane as his successor, perhaps with a little coercion from the Duke of Northumberland. This bypassed the claims of both Mary and Elizabeth to the throne under the terms of the Third Act of Succession laid down by Henry VIII, in which both daughters were legitimised. Jane ruled for only nine days, from 10–19 July, before the Privy Council switched allegiance from Jane to Mary. She and her husband were denounced as traitors and imprisoned. They were both subsequently executed in the Tower of London in February 1554. Darnley was only nine years old when Jane died and she had been dead for twelve years before he married Mary. The story of Jane committing suicide because of Darnley's marriage simply does not fit the facts; it is even doubtful if the two of them ever met. There are those who claim that Lady Jane Dudley was resident at Temple Newsam and committed suicide there, but there is no actual record of this. However, it does leave us with the question of what exactly those serving maids witnessed.

The Blue Lady is perhaps the most famous of all of the Temple Newsam apparitions. People have recorded seeing a hazy blue female figure, or orbs of blue light, in various rooms and places around the house. Even Lord Halifax, the father of the Honourable Edward Wood, claims to have seen this ghostly figure one night. It is supposed to be Mary Ingram, the granddaughter of Sir Arthur Ingram. There is a portrait of her now hanging in the Gothic Room in Temple Newsam House for all to see, and this must have been painted shortly before she died in 1651. The story goes that 14-year-old Mary had been visiting relatives in York. For the occasion she was wearing a beautiful necklace that her grandfather had given her. On the way home, somewhere near the village of Garforth, her carriage was waylaid by either a lone highwayman or a band of thugs, depending upon which version of the story is being told. Whichever it was, the outcome was that she was robbed of all her possessions, including her favourite necklace. She managed to break free from her attackers and ran the rest of the way home to Temple Newsam, about 3 miles away. Arriving home, she was distraught and was put straight to bed. The experience left her deeply traumatised. She trusted nobody and jumped at every shadow and noise. Her behaviour started to grow strange. Sometimes she was to be found picking cushions apart as if looking for something. She scuttled timidly around the house, taking her possessions and hiding them in secret places that only she would know, under floorboards and in walls. Her paranoia grew and she retreated more into herself. She spoke little and refused to eat. She was beginning to waste away and, despite all the efforts of doctors, in a matter of weeks she had died. It is her ghost that is supposed to have been seen, in her blue dress, endlessly searching for the possessions that she had hidden away. Unlike the story of the White Lady, we do know that Mary Ingram actually lived at Temple Newsam House and that she did fall prey to a robbery of some kind. During a period of renovation in the house a few years ago, some small pieces of jewellery and other objects were found beneath floorboards and in a wall.

This time, the facts do support the story and perhaps Mary Ingram is still searching for her hidden possessions.

Another infamous 'ghost' associated with Temple Newsam is that of Phoebe Gray. After the victorious Battle of Blenheim in August 1704, there were many celebrations throughout the country. At Temple Newsam there was to be music, dancing and feasting. Phoebe was a lively and pretty 16-year-old serving girl, some sources say a nursemaid, and was looking forward to the celebrations, as any teenager would. Working below stairs with her as a general servant was a William Collinson. He was older than Phoebe and was very rough and ready. His ill manners and disreputable behaviour meant that he was not the most popular of servants. However, he had had his eye on Phoebe for some time and perhaps he saw the festivities as an ideal time to make a move on her. The story is that Phoebe was taking a hot drink to Nanny Backhouse upstairs in the nursery (now the site of the Bullion Room); something she did last thing every night. This day was no different, despite the festivities. It was late and it was dark, and the way from the kitchens downstairs to the nursery was by a poorly lit stone staircase. Candle in one hand and hot drink in the other, Phoebe made her way up the stairs. Collinson knew her routine well and was lying in wait for her. Drink had made him bolder and, as he hid in the shadows, he imagined what Phoebe and he would be doing shortly. As Phoebe hurried past he jumped out at her. Some say that he only wanted to steal a kiss; others that he intended much more. She screamed and struggled in his arms and then went limp – he had killed her. He later claimed that in trying to stop her screaming he had placed his hand across her mouth and had accidently smothered her; he had not intended to. In a panic, and not knowing what to do, he remembered there was an old Tudor well near the kitchens. Carrying and dragging the dead girl's body along the dark and deserted passages, he heaved off the iron grating covering the well and proceeded to drop poor Phoebe in. He then made off into the night and left the body to be discovered by other staff the next morning. Realising that Collinson was missing, they set out to search for him and he was discovered in a drunken state in an inn in the nearby village of Rothwell. He was arrested and taken to York Prison, the site of the present York Castle Museum. He was brought to trial before the York Assizes and found guilty of Phoebe Gray's murder. He was subsequently hanged on York's Tyburn gallows, situated outside the city walls at the Knavesmire, very near the present-day racecourse. The site of the gallows is now marked by a small paved area and a plaque. Members of staff working late at night in Temple Newsam have said that they have often heard the sound of muffled cries or of something being dragged along a passageway. Occasionally there has also been heard a distant splash, as if something has been dropped into water. All of these occur in the area where Phoebe was said to have been murdered. It is also said that William Collinson himself has been seen skulking in the passageways at dead of night, but sightings have been rare.

K. Goor (2006) also cites two other baffling 'happenings' that have taken place in specific rooms in the house. In the Grey Room, which is situated upstairs in the west wing, between the Darnley Room and Sir John Ramsden's Dressing Room, people have often reported that they can smell smoke. Where the smoke may be smelt by one person in a group, the others will report nothing at all. Those that do experience this say that it smells like pipe or cigar tobacco. Smoke detectors placed around the house have never detected anything unusual. Another room mentioned is Room IV, where a door seemingly opens and closes at will. Other information given is a little more speculative. This room is on the ground floor but Goor makes reference to people hearing noises from the room below, as if furniture is being moved to create a space for dancing. The space below the current Room 4 (IV) was originally the Tudor kitchens but, after they were moved to the north wing in the late eighteenth century, it became the Brushing Room and other storage space. Certainly these were not rooms for dancing in. The only large spaces suitable for dancing would have been either the Great Hall or the Picture Gallery. The rooms above the Hall are numbered in the 20s and the rooms above the Gallery are administrative offices and storerooms, not open to the public. As far as can be ascertained, Room IV has always been situated on the ground floor since it opened to the public in 1923. So, once again, the facts do not always match the story.

So, is Temple Newsam the most haunted house in Yorkshire? Well, certainly there has been an abundance of curious and extraordinary 'happenings' around the house over the years. Some of them are few and far between and may be the products of fertile imaginations; stand by yourself in any room in the house and it is quite easy to let your imagination wander. Other sightings seem to confuse fact and fiction, but should we discount them out of hand? The better known and often cited experiences are based on historical people and recorded facts, such as the attack on Mary Ingram and the murder of Phoebe Gray. More recent unexplained events have been simultaneously witnessed by staff, but they are quite at ease in the house. Cynics may say that there has to be a rational explanation for all of these 'happenings', but if you talk to the staff who work there, they are sensible and sincere in their accounts. Something inexplicable did happen. Ghosts? It is not for me to judge – but I do feel that history is all around us and that, in such an historic place as Temple Newsam, it may be possible that we share time and space with the past.

It is a well-known fact that old houses creak and groan, especially if there is a lot of wood in the construction. Julie Holroyd acknowledges this and has said that there have been many times when she has stood alone in the Great Hall and heard creaks like distant footsteps or doors opening. She knows that this is just the house 'breathing' but she also accepts that there is often a feeling in the house, as if other people are living there as well. She doesn't find this scary; more intriguing, that she is sharing the space with others who have gone before her. If you make a visit to Temple Newsam, take time to stand a while, alone if possible, and see if you experience this as well.

Chapter 10

A Caring House

Temple Newsam as a First World War hospital

When Edward Frederick Lindley Wood inherited the Temple Newsam estate from his aunt in 1904 he was still a young man of twenty-three. He was not a Yorkshireman by birth but was born in Devon, the fourth son of Charles Lindley Wood, the 2nd Viscount Halifax. The Viscount was a fervent Anglo-Catholic, something that his son would continue to have support for, and he often allowed his religious principles to influence his politics. At the second reading of the Matrimonial Causes Bill in 1914, he was very much against giving women equal rights in the matter of divorce:

> The real substance of the Bill is to put women on an equality with men in regard to reasons for divorce; as you increase the facilities for divorce, exactly in that degree do you degrade in public estimation the sanctity and the obligations of Christian marriage. And when you degrade the sanctity and obligations of Christian marriage, you have taken a very serious step to imperil the security and the safety of the family; and since the family is the foundation of the State, anything that touches the security and the safety of the family ultimately affects the security of the State. On that ground – although there are many other grounds why I oppose this Bill – ... I most strenuously oppose any addition to the facilities of divorce.
>
> (House of Lords Debate, 28 July 1914, vol. 17, cc. 189–225)

As a boy, the Honourable Edward Wood grew up in this strict religious background in the family houses at Hinckley Hall near Doncaster, or at Garrowby Hall near York. He was a sickly child, like his older brothers, and had been born with no left hand and a withered left arm. However, this did not stop him enjoying an active life and he went on to participate in hunting and shooting, as well as seeing active service during the First World War. Educated at Eton and Oxford, by 1904 he was an extremely wealthy and eligible bachelor of good pedigree.

As the country slipped gently into the twentieth century, life at Temple Newsam continued as before. Lords, ladies and royalty still made social visits on occasions, and the young Edward was pleased and honoured to receive them. In October 1906, the Princess Louise, daughter of Queen Victoria, and her husband the Duke of Argyll, stayed with Edward for a short period. Other notable visitors included Lord Curzon of Kedlestone and the Lord and Lady Burghclere, both in 1909. In July 1908, the Marquis of Londonderry was invited to speak at a demonstration of the Primrose League, hosted by the Honourable Edward Wood at Temple Newsam. The Primrose League had been founded in the late nineteenth century with the specific purpose of spreading and maintaining Conservative principles and values. Edward Wood, like his father, was a staunch Conservative and would later become the Member of Parliament for Ripon until his elevation to the Peerage in 1925 on the death of his father, his three elder brothers having died prematurely. He was to become one of the most senior Conservative politicians of the 1930s and held several important positions, including Viceroy of India, Foreign Secretary and, in later life, the British Ambassador in Washington. On the resignation of Neville Chamberlain in May 1940, he was popularly expected to become the Prime Minister, but he declined in favour of Winston Churchill.

But life at Temple Newsam was not without its problems. The estate was large and the Leeds Corporation had plans to develop both the water and sewerage systems for the ever expanding city. One of the schemes was to create a sewerage plant in the southern area of the estate, and in 1905, after careful negotiation, it was mutually agreed for Edward Wood to sell 1,000 acres to the Corporation for the sum of £231,000 (a figure approximately worth more than £13 million today). This was not to be the end of the story. The Corporation subsequently made modifications to the plans, before the sale was concluded, and required only 600 acres. This was met with some hostility on the part of Edward Wood and he claimed the land was worth £235,000. The matter rumbled on for some years and eventually went to arbitration under Lord Robert Cecil KC MP and took many days to resolve. Finally, in August 1909, it was agreed that the 600 acres should be released to the Corporation at a price of £149,664 (in the region of £9 million today). The arbitrator may have saved the Corporation over a third of the initial asking price for the land but the estimated total cost of the scheme to the ratepayers, including the costs of the lengthy arbitration, was given in *The Leeds Mercury* of 24 August 1909 as a staggering £1.25 million (approximately £72 million today).

The now wealthier Honourable Edward Wood married the Honourable Lady Dorothy Evelyn Onslow on 21 September 1909 at Clandon Park in Guildford, the seat of Lord Onslow. Their honeymoon was spent in Yorkshire, at Garrowby Hall. After the lengthy childless period of the previous owner, it was not long before Temple Newsam was to hear the cry of children. In July 1910, Lady Dorothy Wood gave birth to twins – Anne Dorothy and Mary Agnes. The newfound joy of the young parents was to be tinged with sorrow as, sadly, within a month, Mary Agnes died. Further children were to follow over the ensuing years: Charles Ingram Wood (1912), Francis Hugh Wood (1916), and Richard Frederick Wood (1920).

For Edward and his new wife and family the future must have felt quite settled. Temple Newsam still hosted various events of quite different natures. In 1910, the estate became part of a sports event when a running race was held in the grounds. By comparison, the Woods also hosted political events such as the meeting of the Castleford Conservative and Unionist Association and the sister Castleford Conservative Women's Association. The house was generously thrown open to the members, who took great delight in examining the many art treasures on show. The house itself was becoming a repository for many fine works. Hidden amongst the various old manuscripts was to be found such gems as a letter from the son of Sir Arthur Ingram written while at Eton in about 1663. Other letters discovered concern the affairs of Sir Arthur Ingram, the Civil War period and the Jacobite Rebellion of 1745; a veritable treasure trove for historians.

All seemed peaceful at Temple Newsam, but dark clouds were gathering. When Archduke Franz Ferdinand of Austria was assassinated in Sarajevo on 28 June 1914, most people in Britain who read of the event reacted with horror.

But they little thought that a brutal action in such a faraway place – a place that many may not even have heard of until then – would have any direct effect upon their lives. There was a prevalent feeling that any political ripples that were caused by the killing would soon be ironed out through statesmanship and diplomacy. Besides, Britain had its own domestic problems to worry about. There was continuing debate over the demand for Home Rule for Ireland; the cotton industry was in decline, with many workers being placed on short time; there was unrest amongst miners in South Wales; and Great Western Rail dining car attendants were on strike. Thoughts of impending conflict were far from many peoples' minds and life continued as normal. In early July, King George V and his queen completed a round of official visits in Scotland. In Leeds there was a meeting of the National Association for the Prevention of Consumption, and the Wesleyan Conference. The outcome of the Cricket Championship contest and preparations for the Great Yorkshire Show seemed important considerations.

However, as July slipped into August, there was a growing feeling of concern. The Stock Market began to stutter and the price of commodities began to rise. The bank rate increased, first to 8 per cent and then quickly to 10 per cent. Foreign travel was also beginning to be affected. On Saturday, 1 August 1914, *The Yorkshire Post and Intelligencer* reported:

> The unsettled state of the Continent is severely interfering with the tourist traffic from this country. People who have booked for the present weekend for Northern Germany and the Rhine are very nervous about going. One hears, for instance, of two parties from the Leeds district which had made arrangements for an educational tour to Lubeck, but which have now cancelled their berths on the steamer. Others who are also contemplating a holiday in Germany are also holding back, though there is no stay in the flow to the Netherlands and even to France.

The same edition reported on the state of the Stock Exchange and increased prices:

> Events moved rapidly in the City yesterday, and a series of sensational events emphasised the seriousness of the financial situation. The Stock

Exchange closed in the afternoon ... and will remain closed until further notice. Then in the early afternoon came a run on the Bank of England, and this was followed by the raising of the Bank rate to 8 per cent. ... Food prices are rapidly rising in Cardiff. Sugar has gone up a penny, butter a halfpenny, bread a penny a loaf. ... At Newcastle yesterday there was a rapid increase in prices for flour, sugar, and similar provisions. ... The prices of ham, flour, sugar, and beef have been advanced in Glasgow. ... Flour is a penny per stone dearer in Sheffield than it was a couple of days ago. Butter is a penny per pound dearer, and sugar a farthing [a quarter of one penny] per pound up. ... In Leeds the price of flour was further advanced by 1s [1 shilling] a sack yesterday, making 3s increase since Wednesday. Flour merchants are inundated with orders from householders anxious to lay in a store before prices get any higher.

What had been a far distant event in an unpronounceable place was now beginning to have a growing impact upon the lives of the general British public. As the time ticked down towards the midnight ultimatum to Germany on 4 August, it became alarmingly clear to many that something tumultuous was about to happen. Long-awaited Bank Holiday railway trips were being cancelled as the trains were put on standby for military transport. The Yorkshire shipping ports of Hull, Grimsby and Immingham were at a standstill. The men of the Leeds Rifles, a Territorial Unit, were rapidly recalled from their training camp in Scarborough, and the three batteries of the Royal Field Artillery Brigade (the 43rd), on training in South Wales, were recalled to their Chapeltown barracks in Leeds. Imminent war with Germany was becoming an increasing reality, although not everyone was supportive. On 4 August, *The Yorkshire Post* carried a full-page advertisement from the Neutrality League, imploring:

BRITONS, DO YOUR DUTY
And keep your country out of a STUPID and WICKED war ...
Ask yourselves; WHY SHOULD WE GO TO WAR? ...
ACT TODAY OR IT MAY BE TOO LATE

Although some in Leeds may have sympathised with the contents of this advertisement, there was a general fervour of patriotism within the city. It was with little surprise that, when they opened *The Yorkshire Post and Leeds Intelligencer* on the morning of 5 August, Leeds citizens read:

ENGLAND DECLARES WAR AGAINST GERMANY
BRITISH ULTIMATUM REJECTED
ARMY AND NAVY MOBILISED
TERRITORIALS EMBODIED
BRITISH RAILWAYS UNDER STATE CONTROL

That fateful day had arrived and Britain was at war. In Leeds, hundreds of young men crowded into the recruiting offices in Hanover Square. By the end of September, 5,000 men from Leeds had joined Lord Kitchener's Army and 1,200 had joined the 'Leeds Pals' Brigade. The reserve battalions of the 7th and 8th West Yorkshires were also almost completely full. When the first group of around eighty wounded soldiers from the Marne battlefield arrived at the Midland Railway station in the city, the reality of war was suddenly there for all to see. Leeds had, in 1908, already been selected as the location of the 2nd Northern General Military Hospital and plans were in place to provide 500 beds in the case of an emergency. The Leeds Corporation almost immediately made available the newly built Training College at Beckett's Park to be requisitioned as a military hospital. It was very quickly adapted and equipped for its new role. By 7 August, 300 beds were in readiness, including 100 at the Leeds General Infirmary, and within two weeks of the declaration of war, the number of beds had doubled to 600, with ninety-two trained nursing staff.

But it was not only some of the British wounded that arrived in Leeds. Within a few weeks of Germany invading Belgium, refugees began to arrive in Britain. The Lord Mayor's Belgian Relief Committee, set up in early September, offered to take 1,000 refugees. Offers of accommodation and assistance from the people of Leeds and the surrounding area were so generous that many more were catered for during the course of the war. The offers were wide and varied. A Major Calverley offered to house and feed twelve refugees at Oulton Hall at his own expense. Although the Hall was unfurnished at the time, he would arrange to equip four bedrooms, a sitting room and a kitchen for their use. Other generous citizens offered to take individual children:

> Mrs Fisher, of Allerton Terrace, Chapel Allerton, Leeds, offering to adopt a girl refugee says: 'I shall never forget the kindly way I was treated by the Belgians when passing through some of the towns which, alas, are now destroyed.'
> 'It is dreadful to think of the poor little children, and it will be a pleasure to me to do what I can for one little child, say between four and eight, until its parents can get a home again,' writes another Leeds lady. There are many such letters.
>
> (*The Yorkshire Evening Post*, 14 September 1914)

Lady Dorothy Wood answered the call as well. She ensured that a number of the Belgian refugees were accommodated on the Temple Newsam estate. These were housed in the stable block for a period. Although Lady Wood was a competent French speaker, she was very confused in that these refugees spoke Flemish, but she was able to contact a Flemish priest in Leeds to assist in translation work. The refugees stayed at Temple Newsam for a long time, during which some of them produced babies. In her *Recollections*, Lady Wood commented that the refugees were well behaved and that the men worked in the gardens or the park, and were very useful and industrious.

Whilst most people saw it as a charitable duty to help the refugees, there were some who felt that a more practical approach should be made towards assisting them:

> The best way of showing practical charity to the brave Belgian refugees would be to find them occupations without delay. Some sympathetic people have endeavoured to heal their wounds by giving them a few coppers; in fact, they have acted towards them as if they were paupers instead of honourable members of one of the bravest nations of Europe. Such charity must cause more grief than relief. Work also is the best grief-killer. Work will keep their brains engaged and this is far better

for them than sitting somewhere idle with the constant vision of the Belgian Drama to gaze at.

(*The Yorkshire Evening Post*, 5 October 1914)

Many of the Belgian refugees did eventually find work, especially in factories that either produced boots or clothing for the military.

It was not only Belgian refugees who were accommodated in Leeds. By the end of October 1914, with the fall of Antwerp, wounded Belgian soldiers began to arrive. *The Leeds Mercury* of 31 October records a 'great reception' for the new arrivals:

Another party of wounded soldiers arrived in Leeds yesterday morning … this being the fourth which has arrived within two days. Yesterday's arrivals were all Belgian soldiers, and numbered about 100. … They received from the large crowd assembled outside the Midland Station a great reception – all the more hearty when it was known that they belonged to the gallant little army which has done so much for the cause of the Allies. About forty of the cases were taken to the General Infirmary, where … there are now about eighty wounded soldiers being taken care of. The rest of the hundred Belgians were taken to the Beckett's Park Hospital.

With the increasing number of war wounded arriving almost daily at the hospitals in Leeds, the service began to find itself stretched. Soldiers who were still in recovery after major treatment, but who no longer required specialist medical attention, were in danger of clogging up the system. They could not be returned to active duties but had to be found a place to recuperate. Owners of country houses in and around Leeds offered their properties as convalescent homes for such patients. Harewood House, Lotherton Hall, Gledhow Hall, Ledstone Hall, and Stapleton Park, among many, were offered as voluntary auxiliary hospitals. Added to this list was Temple Newsam, which officially opened as an auxiliary to the 2nd Northern General Hospital, Beckett's Park, on 29 October 1914. Of the many Belgian soldiers who arrived in Leeds at that time, Temple Newsam took sixteen as the first patients there, and Lady Dorothy Wood was appointed

Commandant. The whole of the south wing of the house was made available as a hospital and the maximum capacity was fifty beds, spread throughout the ground and first floors of the wing.

The Honourable Edward Wood was on active service with the Yorkshire Hussars, at first guarding the east coast before being sent to France. Lady Wood was in charge of the overall administration of the hospital, combining the roles of both Quartermaster and Commandant. She had a staff of a matron and two trained nurses. However, these nurses seem to have created a few problems:

> They frequently stayed out and got drunk, and we had to wait up until they came in (or were brought in) very much the worse for wear.
> (*Lady Dorothy Wood Recollections*, Vol. *The Wars Borthwick Institute*)

Five Voluntary Aid Detachment (VAD) nurses, whose duties included basic work such as cleaning, cooking, setting trays, lighting and maintaining fires, and helping to dress and undress the patients, were on her staff. Lady Dorothy's household staff also assisted the VADs where necessary and a Doctor Bean, living locally in Crossgates, visited regularly. Lady Wood was not actively involved in nursing duties herself:

> I never did any nursing, as the VADs were all passionately longing to try their skills, and I had no wish to do anything in that line. But running the whole show was pretty well a full-time job, and I also worked on the Lord Mayor's War Committee and the Women's Land Committee in Leeds.

As her chauffeur had been sent to France and the car had been requisitioned for war use, getting into Leeds was something of a problem. However, an ancient dog cart was discovered on the farm and a farm hand was always ready to drive her into the city when required.

As the war progressed, Temple Newsam took in British soldiers as well as its original Belgian intake. Again, in her *Recollections*, Lady Dorothy recalls some of them:

The Irish were the worst, but always the most beguiling and full of repentance. The Welsh I thoroughly disliked; they were insubordinate and unpleasant, especially the miners – whereas all the other miners were charming.

As well as receiving treatment to aid their convalescence, the wounded soldiers would have been able to take part in a wide variety of activities provided for them. The main entrance hall at Temple Newsam was turned into a recreation room. A billiard table was provided, as was a piano. There were books to read and board games, and Lady Dorothy herself supervised cinematographic evenings. Visiting entertainers gave performances of various kinds; there were choral groups, soloists, music groups, and variety artists. The more physically able men could go sledging in the grounds during the winter and football matches were regularly played. During the summer months, tennis was an option.

It may seem on the surface that life in such a convalescent home was idyllic. Perhaps in comparison to the horrors of war these men had suffered, it was. But recovery was often a long and painful process. The *Journal of Leeds Territorial Hospitals*, dated 6 April 1918, contains a witty and pithy commentary by an anonymous soldier who names himself 'Simon the Subaltern'. It is set out in pseudo biblical form and is in three short chapters: Chapter 1 deals with an account of treatment; Chapter 2 with recovery; and Chapter 3 with advice from Simon the Subaltern. Below are some short extracts from the piece:

Chapter 1
v3   They all did minister unto the needs of Simon the Subaltern, and
        he prospered abundantly.
v4   And in the course of time did his sinus fill in and he did walk again
        upon his leg.
v5   Then were his days joyous indeed, for he was able to partake of
        tea in the cafés of the city, returning unto the hospital to sleep as
        evening approached.

Chapter 3

v2   Put not your trust in Sisters nor in any of the Medical profession. Yea though they beguile thee with fair words and promises of recovery, believe them not, for yet may not thy wound be healing. Remember moreover, that in time past they have been learned in these things to speak to thee, their patient, in falsehoods.

v3   Be not slow to jump in the time of thy dressing for peradventure the Sister may think that she hurtest thee not and perpetrate upon thee further outrage.

v7   Precious on thy bed is a clean sheet, and few there be that get one.

v10   Hide thy box of chocolates beneath a bushel, nor let it shine before the eyes of the staff.

v11   Happy is the man that wangleth asperin and the man that getteth morphia.

v15   Move not the Sister-in-Charge to anger, for she shall do thy dressing and in her hands is the giving of passes.

v17   A little Blarney is a useful thing.

v19   When thou goest out to tea with a VAD think not to keep it secret, for surely it shall be known throughout the hospital.

One cannot help feel that, although perhaps a little cynical at times, the piece was written from personal experience. It does give us a very real feel of what life might have been like in such a hospital as Temple Newsam. Particularly interesting are the references to 'going out'. As their convalescence progressed, soldiers were allowed escorted visits to Leeds. Sometimes these were group organised, with visits to the theatre, music halls or cinemas. Other times they would visit a café and one can imagine the delight of being escorted on such a visit by a young and pretty VAD.

For the VADs, escorting wounded soldiers on visits would have also been a welcome relief from the daily grind of work at Temple Newsam. Voluntary Aid Detachments operated under the auspices of the British Red Cross Society and the Order of St John. Nursing members received a salary, a uniform allowance, travel allowance, food and accommodation. Non-nursing members, commonly referred to as the VADs, received no payment at all, other than for travel, food and accommodation. Often there was friction between the trained nursing staff, who were in the minority in the auxiliary hospitals, and the untrained VADs. The National Council of Trained Nurses of Great Britain and Ireland voiced a protest, given here in *The Leeds Post and Yorkshire Intelligencer* of 11 December 1914:

> The National Council ... places on record its unqualified disapproval of the present organisation of the nursing of sick and wounded soldiers in military auxiliary hospitals ... the standard of nursing for the sick and wounded should be of the highest quality that a grateful nation can provide for men who are risking their lives in the defence of the Empire, and the Council, therefore, most earnestly petitions ... to prevent the expenditure ... on inefficient nursing, and the subjection of the sick and wounded to the dangerous interference of untrained and unskilled women, who have been placed in positions of responsibility for which they are not qualified, greatly to the detriment of the discipline in military auxiliary hospitals, and the general welfare of the sick.

Strong words indeed, but hundreds of women did step forward to volunteer for work in these hospitals and without them the care of the wounded would have suffered. It is estimated that from 70,000 to 100,000 served as VADs at some time during the war. With their distinctive mid-blue blouses, and starched white aprons and bibs bearing a red cross, they became familiar sights during the conflict.

The life of a VAD was quite disciplined and there were many rules and regulations laid down for them. Each new recruit was issued with a paper from the Commandant-in-Chief of the British Red Cross, detailing what was expected of them:

INSTRUCTIONS TO HOSPITAL VADs, JULY 1915

EQUIPMENT
1. Only the BRCS Regulation Uniform, as detailed on Form D7, may be worn, except in the case of Scottish Members, who may wear their own uniform.

2. Uniform should be worn smartly and in a uniform way, and not to suit the taste of each individual. Scrupulous care should be taken to keep it clean and uncrumpled. Aprons must never be longer than overalls. No additions or alterations, such as veils, bow ties, or shirt collars worn over the coat, are permissible.

3. When travelling to a Hospital by train the following should be taken (if travelling in Regulation coat and skirt):-

1 Overall
1 Apron
1 Cap
1 Pair Sleeves
1 Pair Ward Shoes
1 Collar

4. Members living at any distance from the Hospital should not travel to and from their work in their clean aprons and sleeves. A spare apron should be kept for emergencies.

5. Shoes should always be changed before entering the ward. Comfortable, light-laced shoes with low rubber heels are the best.

6. Scissors, safety-pins, and a pencil or pen should always be carried.

PERSONAL

1. Nails should be kept short and clean. Great care should be taken to have no hangnails or scratches on the hands. If the skin is broken, however slightly, it should be covered with gauze and collodion before assisting at an operation or doing a dressing. Carelessness in this respect may lead to blood-poisoning.

2. The hands should be thoroughly washed and a nail-brush used after any dressing, especially before meals. The hands should when possible be immersed in a solution of disinfectant and well greased at night. If at all roughened, gloves should be worn in bed.

3. All powder, paint, scent, earrings, or other jewellery, etc., should be avoided, as the using of such things invites criticism, and may bring discredit to the Organisation.

4. It is advisable to gargle morning and evening, but especially in the evening. Carbolic, 1 in 60; Listerine, 1 teaspoonful to 5oz water; Glyco–Thymoline and water, ½ and ½ to be used.

5. Members should remember that they cannot work well unless taking regular and adequate meals. They also need a long night's rest, and fresh air, combined with moderate exercise.

6. It is advisable to comb the hair with a small tooth comb once a day.

ETIQUETTE

1. Members should stand to attention when the Medical Officer, Matron, Sister, or anyone in authority enters the ward or speaks to them. Correct titles should always be given, such as: 'Sir', 'Matron', 'Sister', 'Nurse', 'Commandant', 'Quartermaster', as the case may be.

2. When Members meet Superior Officers of Detachments other than their own, they should treat them with equal respect when in uniform. It is due to the Organisation, and is not affected by the individual.

3. VAD Members should be prepared to carry out anything they are asked to do willingly and promptly without question. If they want to help their country they should do so in a generous and unselfish spirit wherever they are most needed and in whatever way their help is most urgently required. They must remember that they are part of a very large Organisation, for which they should be careful to win a good name.

4. Members should show courtesy and consideration to one another and avoid all talk and gossip which might lead to unhappiness in another member of staff with whom they are working.

5. They should also adopt the habit of not discussing the work of their Hospital or Members of its Staff when off duty.

6. Any question as to payment of salary, expenses, or accommodation should be referred through the Sister to the Matron.

7. No Member must leave the Hospital to which she is posted without the permission of the Matron.

8. All Hospital rules must be conscientiously adhered to. We count upon our Members to prove that they have a real sense of discipline, and that they are able to withstand any temptations that may be put in their way. They will thus show that England can depend upon her women to help her generously and honourably in the hour of her need.

(British Red Cross Archives)

The British Red Cross holds record cards for First World War volunteers that can be viewed online (www.redcross.org.uk). These give a fascinating glimpse of the women who volunteered for such service. VADs served at hospitals for varying lengths of time and the record cards show that at the Temple Newsam Hospital, or 'Lady Wood's Hospital' as it was sometimes referred to, volunteer members served from as little as a few weeks up to several months at a time, before being posted to another hospital. Some members, such as Marjory Everest (cook) and Constance Tongue (nurse), were later posted to France after their period at Temple Newsam, and Margaret Upton ended her service in South Africa. The ages of the VADs varied. They were not all young women. The youngest volunteer listed as working at Temple Newsam was 18-year-old Iris Wragg (nurse) from Sheffield, and the eldest was Maria Thompson (cook) from London, aged forty-two. Although not all record cards give the ages of the volunteers and it is possible that there may have been older volunteers than Maria at Temple Newsam.

Thirty-three individual VAD members are listed as having worked at Temple Newsam at some time or another during the war. They were largely single women but two married women are shown to have worked there, one as a nurse and one on general services. The larger majority of the VADs had duties that were referred to as either 'nurse' or 'nursing'. Some duties were a little more specific: 'cook', 'kitchen', 'pantry work' and 'care of coats, boots, blues and pack store' also appear. Of the thirty-three, only eleven members came from the Leeds area. VAD members could be posted anywhere they were required. Those at Temple Newsam came from as far afield as the Isle of Man, Ireland, Wiltshire, London and the south of England. There was no guarantee that if you volunteered in your home town that you would serve there as well. One VAD, Katie Tyrrell, although giving her registered address as 'Temple Newsam' was then posted to the Royal Naval Hospital in Portsmouth. One interesting volunteer was Emily Salkeld, who, like Katie, gave her registered address as 'Temple Newsam' and remained there carrying out the duties of 'various – Housekeeper'. Her husband, Harry, had been the Woods' chauffeur until he was posted to France.

Lady Wood, in spite of her titled status, was prepared to 'muck in' with the running of the hospital, something that was widely recognised. *The Gentlewoman* magazine of July 1917 records her work:

> No one woman has set a better example in war working than Lady Dorothy Wood ... she has given up her home of Temple Newsam, an historic old place near Leeds, as a hospital while her husband ... is at the Front. Lady Dorothy reserves only one sitting and bed room for her own use and does all the household work with her own hands. Even the cooking she manages with the help of a little gas stove set up in the pantry adjoining the breakfast room. Without being actually pretty, Lady Dorothy has much brightness and piquancy and is a devoted mother to her family ... of which the youngest is only a few months old.

And again in an article of 11 August 1917, where she is referred to in the title as 'A Brick':

> Lady Dorothy Wood ... is one of the ablest of war workers and has turned her home at Temple Newsam, near Leeds, into a hospital for the wounded. There are few women who will consent to give up their own domestic staff but Lady Dorothy has done it, only retaining a nurse for her small children. She gets through all the cooking herself on a gas stove in the Butler's Pantry.

However, whilst the above articles paint a somewhat heroic and patriotic picture of an aristocratic lady giving up the benefits of her position for the war effort, her own recollections give a slightly different view. She retained two sisters as housemaids for her own use and, talking of these, she writes in her *Recollections*:

Charlotte was remarkably quick and very soon she was not only an efficient housemaid but had also picked up Parlour work, waiting on me, whenever, instead of eating with the hospital staff, which I did habitually, I had private meals in my sitting-room.

Lady Wood continued as Commandant of the hospital for most of the period that Temple Newsam was used as a hospital, with the exception of the latter part of 1916, when she stood down from her duties due to the imminent birth of her son Francis in October. Her duties were taken over temporarily by a Miss Roff. By January 1917, Lady Wood was back in command, as shown here in an appeal in *The Yorkshire Post* of 4 January 1917:

I am re-opening my hospital [it never actually closed during her confinement nor was it actually 'hers'] at Templenewsam [*sic*] next week, and I am very anxious to have a full-sized billiard table for the men. Unfortunately, our own billiard table was given away shortly before war broke out, and there is nothing the men care about more than a game of billiards. I should be infinitely grateful if anyone could lend me one for their amusement during the long dark evenings. We also badly need a bath-chair, and we are most grateful any time for gifts of eggs, tobacco and cigarettes.

Through all the time that her husband was on active service, as well as being the Commandant of the Temple Newsam hospital, Dorothy Wood was an active campaigner on many fronts. Amongst her many involvements, she was an important member of the Lord Mayor's Relief Fund; she supported the role of women in the war through her support of the National Union of Women Workers; she helped set up an appeal for gifts for the wounded in the Leeds hospitals; she appealed for money to send food parcels to Royal Naval Division prisoners of war from Yorkshire; and she was vocal in recruiting for the Leeds Rifles:

The campaign of the Leeds Rifles was carried to Halton last night. … Lady Dorothy Wood, who met with a warm welcome, said she was astounded and delighted to see how both the men and the women had come forward. She had had an opinion – perhaps they would say she was prejudiced – that women were quicker at understanding things than men, and in the present crisis the women had realised exactly what we were up against. She thought the men were a little slower. At any rate, that was the only explanation she could see why there were some young men who had not yet enlisted. They need have no doubt that they were needed. The war was not nearly over and there was a place for everyone. We had been nearly a year at war, and she would like us to be in the position, when the first anniversary came, of not having a man free and fit who was not a soldier.

(*The Yorkshire Post*, 10 July 1915)

She was an indefatigable person, and in addition to all her official duties, she still found time to act as hostess when required. When a French university delegation visited the city in 1916, she invited them to tea at Temple Newsam. The visitors were able to look at the fine collection of pictures there; the Leeds City Art Gallery had also sent its collection to be housed at Temple Newsam for safety during the war. They were also able to examine the hospital set-up in the house.

By October 1917, the Honourable Edward Wood, now a major, was recalled to England to take on administrative work in London. On 30 October, it was announced in *The Yorkshire Post* that:

Templenewsam [*sic*] Hospital, Leeds, will be closed at the end of November; Major the Hon. E. Wood is shutting up the house and moving to London. The hospital had been a success from the very beginning, thanks to the sympathetic and able management of Lady Dorothy Wood, and it was a most pleasant duty to direct the attention of the Association [West Riding Territorial Association] to the excellent services that she had rendered.

Temple Newsam Auxiliary Hospital closed its doors on 23 November 1917, although the war would continue for a further year. Through the efforts of Lady Dorothy Wood and her staff of VADs, according to W.H. Scott (1923), a total of 615 wounded soldiers had been given respite at Temple Newsam throughout its operation. The Wood family moved to London and the house was shut up and left in the hands of a caretaker staff.

The end of the war brought great social changes. The landed gentry were no longer to be the dominant class. Many landowners faced financial difficulties and houses and land were sold off to recoup growing post-war debts. The Wood family were no different and Temple Newsam was about to move into its final chapter of history.

Chapter 11

A People's House

*After the First World War – Temple Newsam
in public ownership*

Although the Wood family had moved from Temple Newsam in 1917, the house was to remain in their possession for a few more years. A small caretaker staff remained in the house and Lady Wood's personal diaries (held at the Borthwick Institute in York) record that she and her husband made periodic visits through the period 1918–22. Some of the visits were associated with official duties in Leeds and other Yorkshire towns, or were visits made while they were at the family home in Garrowby.

In post-war Britain there was now a feeling of great relief that the hostilities had ended and there was a renewed optimism for the future. But this was a future of change; war had changed the very nature of society. The old order was being shaken; people challenged the validity of the aristocracy. Those men lucky enough to have returned from the war were questioning what they had fought for. Had the sacrifices made been only for a return to the status quo? There was a strong mood of egalitarianism across the country. For many of the landed gentry, the costs of maintaining their estates and houses were becoming untenable. The burden of taxation was immense and many large country houses were either sold or closed up. On 20 September 1922, *The Portsmouth Evening News* carried this article:

AN HISTORIC SEAT
Given Up Through Burden of Taxation
The Hon. E.F.L. Wood, MP, yesterday formally handed over his seat, Temple Newsam, near Leeds, to the Corporation of that city … the Corporation has agreed to pay the nominal sum of £35,000 for the mansion, its treasures, and the estate. Mr Wood said … his decision to

offer Temple Newsam was not reached light-heartedly, but the burden of taxation had become so severe that it was increasingly difficult for him to maintain the estate as it deserved, and had been maintained hitherto. … 'In such circumstances … I felt what the late Mrs Meynell-Ingram felt, that if change there had to be there was one party to who the first offer of Temple Newsam ought rightly to be made, namely Leeds. … The past owners of Temple Newsam have been proud of the traditional connection between their residence and the ancient Order of Knights Templar. I have no doubt that the Corporation and citizens of Leeds will value those associations no less highly.' … He hoped and prayed that Temple Newsam would long be a source of enjoyment and happiness to the people of Leeds.

Contrary to the article above, the Leeds Corporation bought the mansion and the estate but many of the 'treasures' were sold off by auction on 26 July and the three following days, and on 31 July and the following two days. Conducted by a firm of London auctioneers, on instruction from The Honourable E. Wood, the sale was constructed over seven categories:

The contents of the North Wing and part of the Red Passage
The remainder of the Red Passage and contents of the South Wing Bedrooms
The Blue Corridor and the Picture Gallery
Decorative pottery, Chinese porcelain, Bronzes, Chests etc.
School-room, Steward's Room, Ground Floor corridor, Entrance hall and Domestic Offices
Principal Reception Rooms and small collection of pictures
Pewter, copper articles, domestic china, kitchen and laundry effects.

In total, there were 1,457 different lots for sale, ranging from a self-portrait attributed to Rembrandt and a Holbein portrait of Henry VIII to a humble length of rubber hose. Some of the prices fetched seemed to have been relatively inexpensive. In the auction catalogue someone noted (or perhaps paid) the following:

Six + two elbow painted Hepplewhite chairs
  £4 – 5s – 0d (approximately £100 today)
Two mahogany frame Chippendale chairs, seats and backs in red rep
  28s (approximately £30 today)
[Rep is a wool or cotton material used in upholstery.]

The Times of 10 August gave a more detailed breakdown of some of the more desirable treasures on sale. They noted that much of the antique furniture was bought by London dealers. The top price paid appears to have been 1,300 guineas (approximately £30,000 today) for a Queen Anne walnut suite of eighteen chairs and three settees. The attributed portrait of Henry VIII sold for 105 guineas (£3,000 today). In total, it was recorded that the sale raised £14,175 (a little over £300,000 today).

So, after almost 1,000 years of religious, royal and then private ownership, Temple Newsam came into public ownership of the then Leeds Corporation. It immediately advertised for a housekeeper and appointed a Mrs Pawson, and then made plans for the future. One of its earliest ideas was that:

In all probability, work will be provided for the alleviation of the unemployed in the autumn by the construction of a full course of eighteen holes and another of nine holes on the Temple Newsam estate.
(The Yorkshire Evening Post, 5 August 1922)

Golf was extremely popular at this time and the new courses at Temple Newsam were to join the existing municipal courses at Roundhay Park and Gledhow Park. The Temple Newsam courses became quite famous throughout the years and many national and international golfers played there. It was even suggested at one point that the Ryder Cup could be held there. Nothing seemed to stop the golfers. Even in the harsh winter of 1927, when much of the country was covered in snow, it was reported that the hardy golfers of Leeds were playing the course with red golf balls.

It appears that the Leeds Corporation was very keen to use the development of the estate to ease the problem of unemployment in the city. In November 1922, the Council put forward a resolution to link Temple Newsam to the city by a light railway. The following year the General Purposes Committee considered new schemes of relief work for the benefit of the city's unemployed. These included the cleaning out of the three ponds at Temple Newsam and the building of retaining walls for the bridge, and the construction of a light railway from Knostrop Sewage Works to Temple Newsam.

It was intended that the house be opened to the public at some time in the autumn of 1923. Before this could be done, the Corporation had to ensure that there were enough 'attractions' within the park itself. Facilities for the intended masses were an important feature and in January 1923, it invited applications for:

> The privilege of selling ICES on the TEMPLE NEWSAM ESTATE. The person whose offer is accepted will be required to construct a kiosk in accordance with a design to be approved by the Corporation, and the structure is to be placed in such position as the Corporation may determine.
>
> (*The Yorkshire Post and Leeds Intelligencer*, 27 January 1923)

It was also the intention of the Corporation that part of the stable block should be converted into refreshment rooms, where light refreshments would be provided. In previous times a visit to Temple Newsam would have meant a walk around the parkland or maybe, if invited, a tour of the house. Now the Corporation clearly wanted to make Temple Newsam a major city attraction that would draw the crowds. Visitors would also be able to see a fur farm, set up near the Colton entrance to the grounds. Almost 1,000 rabbits were being bred for their fur by well-known local rabbit fanciers Mr Beattie and Mr Wilson. It was hoped that, by the end of the year, there would be a stock of 6,000 rabbits, although I am sure that younger visitors were shielded from the truth of the rabbits' ultimate fate. Another short-lived project by the Corporation was the housing of a small menagerie within the walled garden. There had been a plan to house at least one lioness within the menagerie but this seems not to have happened. *The Leeds Mercury* carried an article by Dr Chalmers Mitchell, of the Zoological Society, who spoke about the rearing of lionesses in England. It appears that a lioness at the zoo (in London) had recently eaten all but one of her cubs due to her cage being boarded off. Mitchell commented:

A hidden lair in a big rocky, cavernous, open-air cage at Temple Newsam, had the Leeds zoo plan been adopted, might have brought better luck.

(*The Leeds Mercury*, 14 April 1923)

It seems that the proposed zoo was little more than a 'petting' zoo, which included the rabbits of the fur farm, and did not contain many of the exotic animals that we would expect to see in a zoo today. By November 1923, the 'zoo' had ceased to exist, when the last few animals were removed, as recorded here in *The Leeds Mercury* of 27 November:

The transferring of two red deer and a badger from the fur farm at Templenewsam to Roundhay Park, yesterday, proved both a difficult and exceedingly hilarious task, and it was only after a strenuous tussle that the animals were captured and taken to Roundhay. Billy, the 2-year-old deer, was not to be coaxed from his lair and would not budge until at last someone went into the hut and pushed him from behind. Then he came into the open. The rope was drawn tight, and four strong men did their best to draw the deer into the crate. A short tussle and he was in. The rest seemed easy, and the captors relaxed their vigilance. Suddenly there was a crash; and in a second Billy had sprung into activity, lashing out with his hind legs, and butting with his head. ... Only after a tussle lasting the best part of an hour was the animal finally stowed safely in his case. Jennie, the other deer, was rather frisky, but she was never allowed to escape, and soon her crate stood beside Billy's on the lorry. The badger gave no trouble. And the three last inhabitants of the Templenewsam Zoo went on their way.

The Corporation also experimented with dairy farming at Temple Newsam. The milk produced was sent to the city hospitals. However, there was some unrest about this at the Leeds Chamber of Trades Council in February 1923. Some members saw this as 'municipal trading' and feared that this, and further possible 'municipal trading' on the estate, was injuring other rate-paying traders. A protest was sent to the Corporation.

Temple Newsam House finally opened to the public on 19 October 1923. The opening ceremony was conducted by the Minister of Labour, Sir Montague Barlow. He made the comparison that, if the Thames was liquid history, then Temple Newsam was a petrified epitome of England. He congratulated the Leeds Corporation on the acquisition of such a treasure house and said that industrialism was driving out beauty and that it must be brought back. The event was covered nationally and the *Derby Daily Telegraph* of 19 October likened Temple Newsam to Hampton Court as a serious rival. It went on to say:

> Its books, pictures and antique furnishings are valued at some £10,000, and are now the property of the Corporation of Leeds. ... There is a herd of cattle in the park belonging to the Corporation, and a scheme is on foot to establish a model municipal dairy farm there.

The public opening was a great attraction and many people did visit both the house and the surrounding parkland in the following years. However, things were not all plain sailing. In 1925, three years after the Corporation took control of the estate, it was reported in *The Portsmouth Evening News* that heavy losses had been sustained during those years. The amount was recorded as £17,000. Much of this loss had been the result of the Corporation's poor efforts at farming on the estate. Even the popularity of golf could not stop municipal losses. *The Athletic News* of 8 August 1927 made the observation:

> The municipal links in Leeds do not pay – yet ... Sir Charles Wilson, Chairman of the Temple Newsam Committee, informed me quite frankly that municipal golf in Leeds does not pay. ... 'The annual expenditure on the links,' he added, 'is greater than the income but I am convinced that municipal golf will be a paying proposition in a few years.'

The financial year ending 31 March 1927 showed that the Corporation spent £62,158 (more than £2 million today) on the maintenance of parks in the city, of which Temple Newsam was one, and a further £10,073 (more than £300,000 today) specifically on the house. This was reported in *The Yorkshire Post and Leeds Intelligencer* on 22 August.

The latter end of the decade saw a tragedy. On 29 December 1928, *The Northern Daily Mail* reported:

> Dismissed from her employment with fifty other girls on Christmas Eve, Marjorie Regan (eighteen) ... was yesterday found drowned at Temple Newsam. In the girl's handbag was found a letter from her employers testifying to her good character.

It had been a successful but difficult decade for the Corporation, but early in 1930 it was proposed that the Yorkshire Agricultural Society's annual show, the Great Yorkshire Show, be held at Temple Newsam. When this was confirmed in October 1931, there was much jubilation in the city. There was no reason to doubt that, given the year-on-year increase in visitor numbers, Temple Newsam would be an ideal location for the show. The Great Yorkshire Show was, and still is today, a prestigious event and always draws large crowds. The date was set for 12–14 July 1932, and all efforts were now geared towards making this event a huge success for both Temple Newsam and the city.

The year 1932 saw a wave of activity focused on Temple Newsam and the forthcoming show. Organisation began in the January, as *The Yorkshire Post and Leeds Intelligencer* of 20 January reports:

> 'Make Leeds talk and think of the Show for the next months.' This advice was tendered ... for the visit of the Great Yorkshire Show to the city next July. ... The Show, as it was the oldest in the country, had grown greatly in dimensions, and the one at Temple Newsam ... would occupy an area of over 40 acres; 750 tons of timber would be used in the construction of the stands; 3 miles of piping would be laid down for the supply of water; the canvas covering the stands would stretch out to 10 miles; and there would be over 4,000 exhibits ... special facilities would be given for school children to attend [in fact, schools were closed on one specific day of the show]. A good thing too was to have tickets sold at reduced rates in advance among the workshops, so that, wet or

fine, the Show was assured of a good 'gate'. ... The Show would bring thousands of visitors to the city.

It was traditional that the local community hosting the show should raise a special fund. For the Temple Newsam show it was set at £2,000. This was to be raised by subscriptions and donations. The fund was to assist with the allocation of prizes across forty categories. However, by June there was still a shortfall of £600 on this target figure. Even just one week before the show opened there was still a deficit of £480. Fortunately for the Corporation an anonymous donor made up the deficit after the show. Admission prices had been set and widely advertised in the press. The entrance for the first day was to be five shillings; the second day two shillings and sixpence, and the third day two shillings, with children at half price on each day. Tickets bought in advance were set at four shillings, two shillings, and one shilling and sixpence respectively. There was also a special tram fare from the city centre to the show set by the Corporation. On the outward journey to Temple Newsam up to 4.30 pm, the fare was set at fourpence from City Square and threepence from the Corn Exchange, with a similar fare on the return journey to the close of the show (at 8.00 pm on each day). These fares were set at one penny above the normal tariff, which would come into operation on the outward journey after 4.30 pm.

The show was a huge success, even if a little on the muddy side. The police were in attendance but only one case was brought to the attention of the courts. A John Dawson, a well-known pickpocket, was found guilty of attempting to steal a cheque book and a watch at the show. He was sentenced to eight months' detention. The Duke and Duchess of York attended the show on the first day and there were attractions of many kinds in the timber town that had been constructed on the estate. Animals of all descriptions could be seen; the latest agricultural machinery was in abundance; and there were demonstrations of various country crafts. Military bands played and there were parades of varying degrees. One notable one was a parade of around sixty pit ponies and pit boys from the South and West Yorkshire mines, and the Duchess, by all accounts, was particularly interested in them. The show, being muddy underfoot, also encouraged a few entrepreneurs:

The shoeblacks reaped something of a harvest after the show. A good many people whose footwear was besmirched with Temple Newsam mud were anxious to have their shoes made a little more presentable. And the shoeblacks were there, waiting at the tram stops in the city. One enterprising 'firm' had a bucket of water the better to get rid of the mud before getting down to the actual polishing process.

(*The Leeds Mercury*, 14 July 1932)

The attendance across the three days was given as 48,648. This was the highest attendance at the Great Yorkshire Show to date and many who visited the show also took in a tour of the house. As well as being a success as an agricultural show, the event put Temple Newsam on the map. Visitors had come not only from across the county but also from across the country. Temple Newsam was now well and truly a tourist attraction. From October 1923, when the house first opened to the public, to September 1932, it was recorded that the house had received 835,353 visitors. Of this number, 350,528 were Leeds residents.

After the show came the great clean-up. The timber buildings were dismantled and reduced to somewhere near half a million strips of timber. These were sold off at auction in the August and timber dealers from all over the north of England attended. An almost disastrous fire broke out in a 20-ton stack in Home Farm in the early hours of 14 August. It was extremely lucky for the show that this did not happen a month earlier. The Leeds Fire Brigade struggled for three hours to bring the blaze under control and to save the surrounding stacks and farm buildings.

The grounds were gradually returned to their former glory as people still came to visit the house and estate. In December 1932, it was announced that a new Rose Garden would be opened to the public in the following year. Planned to cover around 3 acres, it would contain thousands of roses. It was hoped that this, together with the historic house, would draw even more visitors to the estate. Royalty also gave their seal of approval to Temple Newsam when, in August 1933, Queen Mary paid a surprise visit to the house and was very impressed by the arrangements for its public inspection. To add to the spectacular setting of the house and gardens, the Leeds

Corporation Gas department decided in October 1933 that the house would be floodlit on three sides for several weeks.

If the 1920s had been a difficult time for Temple Newsam, then the 1930s were more the golden years. But war was looming once again. Preparations for war were begun early in 1939. In April it was reported that twenty leather buckets in Temple Newsam, dating from the eighteenth century, were to be filled with sand and used in the event of an incendiary attack. By the August, small and valuable exhibits were being packed away ready for storage. When war was declared in September, Temple Newsam House was temporarily closed to the public so that pictures and china from the Leeds City Art Gallery could be moved there for safekeeping. It was decided that these should be placed on display in certain rooms of the house. Towards the end of September, it was announced that the house would be reopened from 1.30 pm until dusk and that there would no admission charge. Defensive sandbagging was to continue around the house, and the cellars were to be made available to the public in the event of an air raid.

On 11 November 1939, Temple Newsam House was officially reopened by Lord Harlech, Regional Commissioner for Civil Defence. *The Yorkshire Post and Leeds Intelligencer* of 13 November gave a full report:

The mansion has been furnished with period furniture as a museum of decorative art. A suite of rooms during the war will house the more valuable contents of Leeds Art Gallery. He also inaugurated an exhibition of the works of art acquired during this year for the Art Gallery and Temple Newsam: 'Temple Newsam is for Leeds, or should be, what Hampton Court is for London – an historic building in lovely surroundings where it is possible to have a display of the arts and crafts of England, in a setting worthy of them and your great city. ... It is my hope that, even in wartime, Leeds City Council may find it possible to continue its contributions and add to what is already a notable and distinguished collection of which the citizens should be proud. ... A city like Leeds can, through its support of the Art Gallery and Temple Newsam and all they now stand for, do much for the real progress of civilisation of our country.'

Throughout the war, Temple Newsam House became the home to many nationally important exhibitions of artwork. From 1939 to 1945, there were exhibitions of Chinese work, French art and modern art, sculpture by Epstein, and the paintings of Walter Sickert, Augustus John and Wilson Steer. Visitor numbers increased in spite of travel around the country becoming more difficult. The war seemed to have had very little impact upon the house; in fact, it could be argued that its role as a venue for art exhibitions enhanced its reputation and paved the way for its status today. There was only one relatively minor incident reported, in August 1940, when a fire was discovered in an empty room from which exhibits had recently been removed for the floor to be polished. The fire was quickly put out by staff, with only minor fire damage to the floor and discoloured panelling. Fortunately, a valuable Chinese Coromandel screen had been removed from the room only a day or two before.

If the house was not affected by the war, then the estate was. Food production was of prime importance and the Parks Committee put forward a plan to use available land in all of the city parks. In greenhouses it was proposed to grow produce such as French beans and tomatoes, and many flower beds would be given over to the growing of vegetables. The rose gardens at Temple Newsam and at the Roundhay Park Canal gardens were to be spared for the continued enjoyment of the public. Pigs were kept on the farms at Temple Newsam and Skelton Grange. In total, there were about 300 pigs; they were fed from waste produced by works canteens across the city and from household scraps put out for collection. There was also a scheme to put bins in every school so that children could deposit waste food, and communal bins were to be sited around the city. The Council also sowed corn and oats in fields on the Temple Newsam estate. It was in connection with one of these oat fields that a somewhat unusual case appeared in court in 1940:

A 19-year-old couple [male and female] ... were summoned in Leeds today for doing malicious damage to growing oats at Temple Newsam. ... One of the fields had been sown with oats, and it was into the field of growing oats, ready for cutting next week, that the two defendants went on the evening of Sunday, 14 July. They went into the standing oats and sat down on a mackintosh, with the result that 28 square feet of the oats was laid completely flat. ... The amount of damage was estimated at £1 10s. It was hard to believe that anyone would behave in such a wanton and reckless manner at a time like the present.

(*The Yorkshire Evening Post*, 1 August 1940)

I would imagine that damaging crops was the last thing on this couple's minds when they laid down their mackintosh. They were found guilty of malicious damage and could, under the letter of the law, have been detained for one month. In this instance they were each fined ten shillings and ordered to pay fifteen shillings damages with seven shillings costs – a rather expensive roll in the oats!

The Ministry of Works and Planning had begun small-scale open-cast coal mining to the south of the estate in May 1942, but in December this was expanded to take in the two municipal golf courses at Temple Newsam. The estimated total tonnage of coal available was 445,000, of which only 53,000 had been taken already. An area of 270 acres of parkland would be involved, including the golf courses, and the ground would be excavated to a maximum depth of 50 feet. There was a natural concern as to how and when the land would be reinstated after the extraction of the coal. The Ministry had a policy of back-filling with sub-soil as the work proceeded, and then replacing the top soil and reseeding. In this way, they claimed the land could be easily returned to pasture in two or three years. The Director of Parks was not entirely convinced. He described the scene, as the giant excavators got to work:

The land is devastated ... as if Rommel and the 8th Army had been over the land with their guns and tanks.

(*The Yorkshire Evening Post*, 9 December 1942)

Two years later, there was still controversy over the restoration of the land. Although some land had been restored and was available again for golfing purposes, there was a great fear that other restoration work would be delayed. Heavy machinery used to restore the land had, for some inexplicable reason, been taken off site. There had been industrial action by miners in nearby collieries and it was suggested that the delays in restoring the land had been linked with this, although there was no direct evidence.

There were accidents and fatalities during the extraction of coal from Temple Newsam. It was hard and difficult work, whether working in an open-cast or underground environment. There were several cases reported in the press, perhaps this one being the most poignant:

> Harry Wood (fourteen) … was fatally injured by coal wagons at the Waterloo Main Colliery's Temple Pit, Temple Newsam, Leeds. The boy was a screen hand, and a train of empty wagons was being shunted in the screen siding when the accident occurred. He had been employed at the pit only seven weeks.
>
> (*The Yorkshire Evening Post*, 18 May 1940)

In terms of actual military involvement, a platoon of the Home Guard was stationed at Temple Newsam and training exercises were held in the grounds.

> Members of the Home Guard, in teams of three, yesterday went through gruelling assault course built by members of a platoon stationed at Temple Newsam, Leeds. The course consists of sixteen hazardous tests. These include overcoming a barbed wire fence, wading through a lake, and swing across a thin but strong rope stretched between two trees about 25 yards apart.
>
> (*The Yorkshire Post and Leeds Intelligencer*, 19 October 1942)

When the war came to an end in 1945, Temple Newsam House stood unscathed. The same could not be said for the surrounding parkland. The open-cast mining had ravaged the southern aspect of the estate and mining operations extended to within 100 metres of the south walls of the house. There were fears that blasting operations were having an effect upon the structure of the building. Minor tremors were felt and cracks had begun to appear in the ballroom ceiling. Deep mining left Temple Newsam House on a pillar of unmined bedrock. But by April 1946, it was being reported that about 400 acres of land had been restored, and more was to come.

With an air of post-war optimism, the Leeds City Council, as it was now called, proposed some ambitious plans for the estate. A sports stadium to accommodate 150,000 spectators, with parking for 1,000 vehicles and sidings for trams was put forward. It was to be the 'Wembley of the North'. At the same time, a memorial peace garden plan was approved for a 50-acre site in the estate. This was to include:

Gardens representative of thirty countries, with appropriate architectural settings. The garden of China for instance … would have a red lacquer pavilion, green dragon, bridge of jade, and so on. … The garden of Holland would have a realistic Dutch farmhouse in the background, the whole fronted by a canal.

(*The Yorkshire Evening Post*, 2 January 1946)

The complete plan was to include an open-air theatre, a large lawn with a raised dais, parking for 100 cars, a day nursery where children could be left, and designated sylvan picnic areas. There was much controversy over these plans and eventually the idea was abandoned. The sports stadium as per the plans did not fully materialise either. A sports arena was constructed in the 1950s, but not to the plans originally put forward. The cinder running track still exists today.

Artworks belonging to the City Art Gallery were returned but Temple Newsam House still retained its status as an exhibition space. There was a programme of purchasing period furnishings, some of which were originally in the house. Donations and bequests also helped make the house a living museum. People still flocked to view the new acquisitions and marvel at the paintings. As the numbers of visitors increased, the Parks Department suggested that a small-scale railway be constructed throughout the park, modelled on the one at Scarborough, so that visitors could be transported around the grounds. This did not appear until early 1960, when the Leeds Society of Model and Experimental Engineers built a narrow gauge railway in the park. They operated it until the early 1970s.

The early 1950s was a time for celebration. The Festival of Britain reached every corner of the land in 1951, and Leeds was no exception. A major exhibition of Chippendale furniture was planned for Temple Newsam as part of the festival. Mary, Her Royal Highness, The Princess Royal and Countess of Harewood, opened the exhibition on 8 June, and the Long Gallery was filled with exquisite examples of Chippendale's work. More than 300 guests attended the opening ceremony. Later in the year, a major travelling Festival exhibition of the works of William Hogarth was also presented in the house. There were concerts and recitals in the house, and open-air theatre and ballet performances in the grounds. More controversially, a Henry Moore modern sculpture, *Reclining Figure*, was set to be displayed in the grounds. With Temple Newsam being more usually associated with 'traditional' artwork, some comments were quite forthright: 'Dump this figure in the lake'; 'What the deuce is it?'; and 'Why have it in the vicinity of our lovely old Temple Newsam House?'

Festivities and celebrations continued into 1952, with the accession of Queen Elizabeth II to the throne, and her coronation in 1953. Early in 1953, Temple Newsam was to embrace modern technology. On 17 February, the house was the subject of a thirty-minute television broadcast by the BBC. Although television was in its infancy, it did bring the architecture and treasures of Temple Newsam to an even wider audience. I am sure that this would have bolstered visitor numbers throughout 1953, and especially to the exhibition of Royal Robes. This was a display of robes worn at the Coronation in Westminster Abbey. The Princess Royal was once again on hand to open the exhibition on 25 July. On 8 August, *The Yorkshire Post* reported:

Yesterday 3,098 saw the exhibition of Coronation robes. ... It is attracting greater crowds than has ever been known at the house before. Since the exhibition opened ... 31,264 people have visited it.

Temple Newsam appeared to be going from strength to strength. Yet, at the same time, it was announced that another stately home of England was to disappear: Dalton Holme Hall, near Driffield, was scheduled for demolition. The owner, Lord Hotham, was no longer able to finance the required repair and maintenance bills to keep the property open. One wonders if this would have been the fate of Temple Newsam had the now Lord Halifax not had the foresight to pass the estate on to the city. For all the trials and tribulations that the Leeds Corporation may have had on taking over Temple Newsam, they were clearly doing something right. Visitor numbers were on the increase.

The programme of redecoration, restoration, and preservation would continue over the following decades. As more period pieces were added to the collections, the house developed a balance between a museum and a representation of a bygone lifestyle. This process of development still continues today.

Milk production at Home Farm continued up until 1968, when the dairy herd was dispersed and the farm ceased operation. For a time in the 1970s, the farm buildings held the stables and kennels belonging to the West Yorkshire Police Force. An indoor riding school was also constructed within the farm. This continued until the late 1970s, when the City Council decided to re-open the farm as a visitor attraction and it was designated as a Rare Breed Centre. It is now one of the largest in Europe and well supported by visitor numbers.

Another creation for the summer of 1979 was the construction of an amphitheatre between the northern face of the house and the stable block. An elongated performance area surrounded by tiers of brick-edged grassy banks was to provide a venue for many theatre companies. Open-air theatre was nothing new to Temple Newsam, but now here was a designated performance space. During the 1980s, the Leeds-based Tinderbox Theatre Company presented an annual summer performance. Over the years, the amphitheatre had become the deck of a ship, in Shakespeare's *The Tempest*, a living farmyard for Brecht's *The Caucasian Chalk Circle* and a Native American Indian encampment for Bogdanov's interpretation of *Hiawatha*. It even became an Italian piazza, complete with working fountain and pizza parlour, for a production of *The Two Gentlemen of Verona*. Come rain or shine, audiences turned out every year.

Temple Newsam now provides a diverse range of events, catering for all ages and tastes. Over the years we have witnessed rock concerts with the likes of U2, Guns 'n' Roses and the Sex Pistols. The City Council has organised *Opera in the Park*, with such stars as Katherine Jenkins, Alfie Boe, and Lesley Garrett. *Party in the Park* has catered for the younger members of our society, as has the *Breeze Festival* and *Cocoon in the Park*. There are fun runs, charity runs, steam fairs, vintage car rallies, dog training, kite flying, model aeroplanes, and seemingly more every year. What is more important is that, in all of this visitor development, the house has not been left behind. Temple Newsam could so easily have become a dusty museum, but it is kept alive by the dedicated work of the staff, who are always willing to engage with the public. Rachel Conroy has been the Curator of Temple Newsam since December 2015. In only a short time she admits that the house 'gets under your skin'. As she explained to me:

> The collection is remarkable in its quality and scope and the house provides an extraordinarily rich and interesting context in which to display and interpret it. I am particularly drawn to the Picture Gallery and Blue Drawing Room (otherwise known as the Chinese Room). They are visually stunning but also encapsulate such interesting stories about the house and its past owners.

It is these stories that have brought Temple Newsam to life, and will continue to do so for future generations of visitors. As we have seen, the Temple Newsam estate has a long history and there are many anniversaries to be celebrated soon: 500 years since the first inventory of Lord Darcy's house (2018); 100 years of public ownership, and 400 years since the house was bought by Sir Arthur Ingram (2022); and a century of the house as a museum (2023). The estate has seen many changes throughout the centuries. It has survived rebellions and wars, it has witnessed the industrial and technological revolutions, and it has seen major social upheavals. Above all of this, Temple Newsam House has stood the test of time and is rightly termed the 'Hampton Court of the North'.

Select Bibliography

Books

Alberti, L.B., James, Leoni (ed.) & Joseph Rykwert (Trans.), *Ten Books on Architecture*, Alec Tiranti Ltd, London, 1955.

Bingham, C., *Darnley; A Life of Henry Stuart Lord Darnley Consort of Mary Queen of Scots*, Phoenix, London, 1997.

Barber, M., *The Trial of the Templars*, CUP, New York, 1978.

Brown, J., *The Omnipotent Magician, Lancelot 'Capability' Brown*, Chatto & Windus, London, 2011.

Close Court Rolls Edward II, HMSO, London, 1892.

Crossley, F.W., *A Temple Newsam Inventory 1565, Yorkshire Archaeological Journal* XXV, 1918–19.

Eyres, P. (ed.), 'Yorkshire Capabilities', *New Arcadian Journal 75/76*, New Arcadian Press, 2016.

Fawcett, R., *The Early Tudor House (Temple Newsam) in the Light of recent Excavations*, Leeds Arts Calendar No.70, 1972.

Goor, K., *Haunted Leeds*, Tempus Publishing Ltd, Stroud, 2006.

Harvey, Dr S. & Holt, J.C. (ed.), *Taxation and the Economy in Domesday Studies*, Woodbridge, 1987.

Hopkins, H., *The Long Affray*, Secker & Warburg, London, 1985.

Jerdan, W., *Rutland Papers. Original Documents illustrative of the Courts and Times of Henry VII and VIII*, John Bowyer Nichols & sons, London, 1842.

Kitson, S. & Pawson, E., *Temple Newsam*, 1931.

Knowles, D. & Hadcock, R.N., *Medieval Religious Houses: England and Wales*, Longman, 1994.

Levy, M.J., *The Mistresses of King George IV*, Peter Owen, London, 1996.

Lomax, J., *Victorian Chatelaine; Emily Meynell Ingram of Temple Newsam and Hoar Cross*, October 2016.

Moore, L. & Pullan, N., *Great War Britain Leeds; Remembering 1914–18*, History Press, Stroud, 2015.

Morton, A.L., *A People's History of England*, Obscure Press, 2006.

Ridley, J., *Henry VIII*, Penguin Books, London, 2002.

Roberts, R., *The houses of Sir Arthur Ingram and Lionel Cranfield, Earl of Middlesex; a comparative study of elite architecture in England 1600–1645*, History Lab seminar, June 2010, IHR, accessed www.academia.edu

Robinson, P., *Leeds Old & New*, Richard Jackson Ltd, Leeds, 1926.

Schama, S.A., *History of Britain Vol 1*, BBC Worldwide Ltd, London, 2000.

Schama, S.A., *History of Britain Vol 3*, BBC Worldwide Ltd, London, 2002.

Scott, W., Sir *Ivanhoe*, Signet Classic, 2001.

Scott, W.H., *Leeds in the Great War*, Leeds Libraries & Arts Committee, 1923.

Stenton, F., *Anglo Saxon England 3rd edition*, OUP, 1971.

Strong, R., *The Renaissance Garden in England*, Thames & Hudson, London, 1979.

Victoria County History, *Houses of the Knights Templar A History of the County of York Vol 3*, London, 1974 London.

Wheater, W., *Temple Newsam; Its History and Antiquities*, A. Mann, Leeds, c1860.

Worth, R.N., 'The Plymouth Company'; *Report and Transactions of the Devonshire Association for the Advancement of Science, Literature and Arts Vol XIV*, W. Brendon & Sons, Plymouth, 1882.

Yorkshire Post, The, 'Leeds and its History'; *The Yorkshire Post Tercentenary Supplement, Yorkshire Post*, 1926.

Some useful websites

www.leeds.gov.uk/museumsandgalleries – for information on Temple Newsam

www.scarletfinders.co.uk – for information of nursing during the First World War

www.britishredcross.org.uk – for information on nursing and access to First World War nursing records

www.britishnewspaperarchive.co.uk – an online searchable database of old newspapers (subscription service)

www.leodis.net – an online searchable database of old photographs of Leeds

www.ancestry.co.uk – possibly the largest and most accessible genealogy website (subscription service, but look out for 'free trials')

www.british-history.ac.uk – for online access to historical documents (subscription service)

www.rbst.org.uk – for information on the Rare Breeds Survival Trust

A note of monetary values mentioned in this book

I am aware that some readers may be unfamiliar with pre-decimalisation money. On 15 February 1971, the old British system of pounds, shillings and pence was decimalised. The pound was then subdivided into one hundred pennies. So, £1 = 100p and values were written as, for example, £5.30 (five pounds and thirty pence).

Prior to this, the pound was divided into twenty shillings (s) and each shilling into twelve pence (d). So, 12d = 1s and 20s = £1. Values were written as, for example, £30 – 4 – 6 (thirty pounds, four shillings and sixpence). For smaller amounts, you may have seen 3s 4d (three shillings and four pence) or sometimes 8/- (eight shillings and no pence) or 7/6 (seven shillings and sixpence).

There is one other unit that is sometimes mentioned, and that is the Guinea. A Guinea was worth twenty-one shillings, or 21/- , or £1 – 1 – 0.

When comparing old and new values, for consistency I have used the currency converter supplied online by the National Archives.

Images
Every effort has been made by the author to locate the copyright holders of images reproduced within this book.

Index